TRAVELS IN RUSSIA

THE FOUR AND A HALF ADVENTURES OF A NERVOUS NOVICE

TRAVELS IN RUSSIA

Text Copyright © 2023 Landers Faraway

All photographs of Russia and diagrammatic maps
Copyright © Landers Faraway

Other images Public Domain

All rights reserved. No part of this publication may be reproduced, stored in any retrieval system or transmitted in any form or by any means, without the prior consent and permission in writing of the author, nor be otherwise circulated in any form of binding or cover other than that in which it is published nor without a similar condition being imposed on the subsequent purchaser.

LandersFaraway@outlook.com
Agent: andyglenthorne@hotmail.co.uk

Paperback ISBN 9798871736500

First Edition November 2023

10 9 8 7 6 5 4 3 2 1

LANDERS FARAWAY

TRAVELS IN RUSSIA

THE FOUR AND A HALF ADVENTURES
OF A NERVOUS NOVICE

A JMB COMMUNITY BOOK

CONTENTS

An Introduction Page 7

Travel By Train Page 13

Travel By Boat Page 73

Travel To Old Russia Page 143

Travel To New Russia Page 187

Travel To Wilderness Russia Page 233

Epilogue Page 247

HOW IT ALL STARTED

AN INTRODUCTION

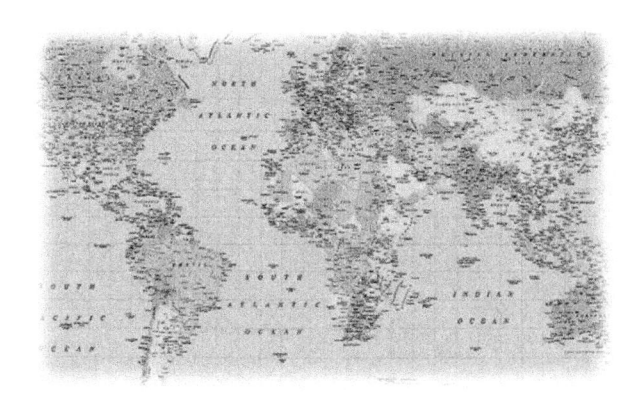

BEGINNINGS

LET ME MAKE CLEAR, before anything else that follows is read, that I am not a travel expert. In fact, as the subtitle to this book suggests, I am the opposite, a complete novice and most certainly, even after the adventures described here, I cannot in any way be regarded as a seasoned traveller. That is especially since I only seriously started exploring foreign lands twelve years ago. In my travels over the last twelve years I have not gone to any remote areas away from human civilization and contact and I have not gone to jungles, deserts, war zones or storm-tossed seas. However, for me each journey has been a leap, a pushing of my boundaries and an adventure, an adventure to places not on the horizon of most people and, as you will find out, all in one direction, that direction being eastward of my home country, the United Kingdom, to very, very ancient lands where borders, cultures and political systems have been subject to huge changes. This book concentrates on my travels in Russia but my curiosity has taken me, over those years, into other countries in eastern Europe as well.

So who am I? I am a middle-aged man, steady, cautious, conservative and quiet. I am not courageous and can suffer from anxiety and the occasional 'black dog' episode, generally drug controlled, but which can cause me to suffer all the difficulties of that condition and can cause my world to shrink down to a very small space. What else? Well, I like a predictable lifestyle so I live in a 1930s semi-detached house in the commuter belt of London. I have had a usually enjoyable 9-5 job but, as you will read, not without issues. I like being looked after by my wife and children, only one of whom - that is, children - remained at home when my adventures started. I am not rich. I am not poor. At parties I stand in the corner and in large groups I am silent. Generally, I take the easy route through life. I don't drink. I don't smoke. I cut my lawn at weekends. I type in Times New Roman. I drive a Honda Jazz.

So, as I said, I am steady, cautious, conservative and quiet.

My wife is in many ways similar although she may not like to hear that. Yet for ages, despite all of the above, I had wanted to live a different life to the one I had lived so far. Some people satisfy their mid-life crises by taking up a sport or changing job or in extreme cases they change spouse. I did none of those things but at the age of fifty I did acknowledge the wanderlust in my genes - but not in my wife's. There was a frustration knowing that there is a big world out there waiting to be explored and I felt the urge and wish to go places, an urge and wish which I had previously suppressed.

The key moment was when a marital difference of opinion led me to say to my wife 'well if you don't want to go travelling do you mind if I go off and do some?' to which she graciously replied 'no, I don't mind' and so with that simple blessing the door to a different world was unlocked for me.

However, would I be daring enough? Would I overcome my fears or would this be a step too far for my anxieties? How 'brave' was I being? Having wanted to travel and explore the world for so long would I enjoy the reality or was my idea of travel an illusion? And where to go? The world is a big place and there is lots of choice. Could I go to the Americas? Too expensive. Australasia? The same. Thailand, India, Sri Lanka? Lovely countries but the diet wouldn't appeal. Africa? Too adventurous. So that left Europe as the most likely destination for my first travels but where, where in Europe?

What follows are stories of where I ended up but hopefully more than that. I love history and so I have included very brief outlines of the historic background to the various places visited as well as giving an indication, but only an indication, of things and places to see, lest I take away the enjoyment and satisfaction of others in finding these for themselves. I have described my preparations. I make no secret of the fact that I make up for my anxieties and lack of courage by over-preparing, by reading, by investigating and by trying to pre-empt any difficulties that may arise. I am full of admiration for those who do go off somewhere not knowing how they will travel or where they will stay but that is not me. I need to have a good plan and I enjoy the planning almost as much as the going. Therefore, I have included elements of that and of how my planning and experience have developed over the years.

Take what follows as you find it. My hope is that this is a 'how to do' as well as a 'what to do' and a 'what I did' book that does not take away the thrill and excitement of discovery and seeing sights for the first time as well as a book which complements the wealth of information available in other travel books and guides and online.

THE VERY FIRST ADVENTURE
TRAVEL BY TRAIN

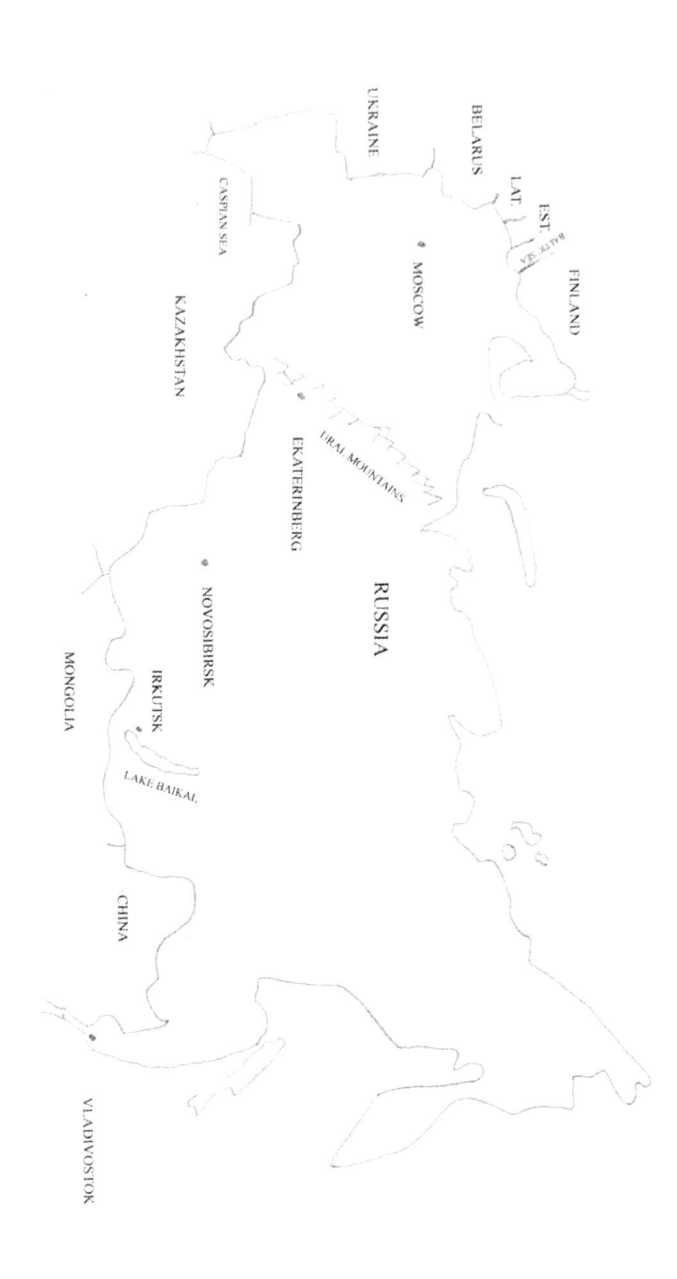

WHERE?

IT'S THE BEGINNING OF the 1980s, a time of huge change in the United Kingdom - the time of Margaret Thatcher, the Falklands War, international tensions with the Eastern bloc and a time of unemployment followed by growing prosperity.

I'm in my early twenties and have been invited as a guest to a social gathering in someone's house. As well as the retired ex-civil servant host and his wife there were ten or so other people of mixed ages, gender and occupation. There were current civil servants, there was a health visitor, an accountant, a teacher, a middle aged South African couple just about to move away to run an orchard business, a bank clerk and me, a surveyor. Some stood and chatted, others took food and sat with plates on laps and drinks on the floor. Sitting on upright chairs to one side of the room was a softly spoken, stooped elderly man, Arnold, and his petite wife, Jenny, afflicted with the curse of dementia, meaning that Arnold couldn't leave her side and was constantly and lovingly tending to her. I worked my way around the room, where possible making conversation, and eventually sat next to them. Our respective ages made chatting a little difficult but since I knew nothing of them except by name I asked Arnold, after the usual introductory courtesies, as to their background. As we talked I became fascinated. Arnold reminisced about his time in China, first as a child of missionaries there and then subsequently a Christian missionary, along with his wife, in his own right. What particularly caught my attention however was his description of the many weeks his parents and he had spent travelling to China across the Russian Empire in the time of the last Czar on a steam-pulled train on the Trans-Siberian Railway. I was awe struck and walked away at the end of the evening thinking 'never under-estimate the old!' I never forgot that conversation.

Now, nearly thirty years later, in 2010, as I looked at a map of the world and wondered where to go travelling that conversation came to mind and without any hesitation I was decided. It was as simple as that. Russia and the Trans-Siberian Railway were calling. However, I knew little of Russia, except that it was big, had lots of snow in winter and had a violent history. That is probably all most people know but browsing on Google I discovered that Russia:

- Is the world's largest country, even after the break-up of the USSR, and covers approximately a tenth of the earth's land mass and spans Asia as well as Europe. It used to be even larger before Alaska was sold to the United States in 1867. Even though it now crosses eleven time zones, including Kaliningrad, its population is only 140-150 million people.
- Has Europe's largest lake by area, Lake Ladoga, and Europe's longest river, the Volga, as well as Europe's highest mountain, Mount Elbrus, in the Caucasus.
- Has the world's deepest, and by volume largest, freshwater lake, Lake Baikal.
- To state the obvious is cold in winter but also, which I hadn't grasped, very hot in summer.
- Had a violent communist revolution in 1917 when the Russian Empire became known as the Union of Soviet Socialist Republics, the USSR, and as the USSR it played a major role in the Second World War which was followed by nuclear stand-off with the West in the Cold War. In 1991, under President Gorbachev, the communist regime collapsed and the USSR fragmented into its constituent countries. Years of chaos followed in rump Russia under President Boris Yeltsin, succeeded by the firm government of President Vladimir Putin.
- And, most importantly for me, it has the world's longest railway, the Trans-Siberian.

So, I had made my decision but that was the easy bit. What do I do now? How do I go about this? I was a complete novice and knew next to nothing. I needed to educate myself about travelling abroad, about Russia past and present, about the Trans-

Siberian Railway and about so many other things. With that in mind the first place I headed to was my local high street travel agent.

As I opened the door to the travel agent's the uniformed lady who met my eye from behind her desk smiled, invited me to a seat and listened receptively as I explained what I was after. She beckoned me to the display shelves and pulled out a few brochures, selected a couple to place in my hand, including an Intourist brochure and a brochure from a really, really luxurious operator, which one I cannot now recall, and kindly said 'Take these, have a look and then come back to us'. With profound thanks I put the brochures in a plastic carrier bag, for discretion, and headed home to study them.

The brochure from the luxurious operator I read with interest and then put aside as offering something several classes above my station in life and where I would be uncomfortable and certainly much, much too expensive. Anything I did would have to be done on a sensible and realistic budget, a budget that gave value for money and which wouldn't crash my bank account. That budget was presently ill-defined but I definitely knew what was too much. Subsequently I would come across many luxury trips that charged a lot. The Intourist brochure I read several times and they seemed to be proposing tours along the same broad idea that I had envisaged. What was apparent was that I needed to study the basics a bit more so I called in to my local council library and borrowed Bryn Thomas's excellent 'Trans-Siberian Handbook' as well as Lonely Planet's 'Russia'. Eventually I bought my own copies of each of these. My family got little sense out of me over the next few days as I read these from front to back. I was on a steep learning curve but began to get a good overview of Russia, it's main cities and towns, its history, its railways and practicalities such as visa requirements, currency, climate, when best to go and so on.

Also, I found out that there was not one Trans-Siberian Railway but for parts of the route several different alternatives, through Perm or Kazan, through Ekaterinberg - English Yekaterinburg - or through Chelyabinsk. There were different destinations, either Vladivostok or turning south through Mongolia to Bejing in China or north onto the Baikal Amur Mainline Railway but all seemed to have Moscow as the starting point, or maybe as the finishing point, for one could go west to east or east to west. I could go six days non-stop or make a number of stops along the way. That meant I would need a minimum of eight days but with any maximum length of tour that I wished. I could go extreme luxury, fully escorted, which on my income would be bankruptingly expensive, or I could go unescorted on local commuter train services.

As a regular commuter on London's train services I rejected the idea of doing the journey in six days non-stop - I was not going so that I could see the inside of a train but to see the scenery, cities and sights - and, as I have said, being on a budget I rejected the luxury option with its high comfort, good food, good service and quality train interior. Also, I decided that it would be nice to be heading towards home, that is, from east to west, rather than away from home and I would not feel that I had completed the journey fully if I did not include Vladivostok and Moscow on each end of an itinerary. Work and home commitments would limit the duration to a maximum of two weeks.

I looked again at a map of Russia and Bryn Thomas's and the Lonely Planet books. Most of the major cities between Vladivostok and Moscow looked really interesting and full of sights worth exploring so I took an evening to compose an e-mail to Intourist. Intourist was the Soviet travel agent through whom all tourism into the USSR was handled. They controlled where and when tourists visited, their itinerary, what they saw, who they spoke to, what they ate and where they slept, even having their own hotels. All foreign visitors were accompanied by an Intourist guide. However, after the fall of communism Intourist entered the world of competitive commercial tourism, the world in which all Western travel agents operate.

As the Intourist brochure explained, as well as packaged tours they offered tailored bespoke holidays and it was this for which, in my naivety, I asked them to price, requesting many, many stops. I feel guilty now at the thought of some poor person spending several hours examining train timetables and accommodation options to give me something which, although very reasonably priced and within my budget, when I studied the detail of their proposal I could not accept. I had not realised that in some locations I would have to wait until the next day or sometimes two days for an ongoing train and that, as I had planned it, the journey would take over three weeks which would not fit in with my work and family commitments. Nevertheless, thank you Intourist for your efforts and for introducing a bit of realism, clarifying my thinking and managing my expectations but now I was back to square one.

What to do now? Pulling the Bryn Thomas and Lonely Planet books off my shelf I selected a couple of the tour companies suggested and turned to Google to check out Just Go Russia (JGR), also known as Go Russia, and Real Russia, both internet-based companies. I spent yet another quiet evening at home browsing their websites. Both seemed good but JGR advertised regular talks on travelling in Russia at a venue in Kensington in London. I put the relevant day in my diary and on a dark, cold January evening went along.

The talk was held in a largish lecture hall which was about a third full with thirty or so people and three JGR staff who showed a film and gave a verbal presentation. They explained that they use the regular train services for their tours which were fully organised, with taxis meeting trains and city tours starting at the relevant hotels, but the journey was unescorted. They then opened up the meeting to questions from the floor. Many were asked including one man enquiring whether the train sleeping accommodation had ensuite bathroom facilities. Now, having read into the subject a little bit, I was an 'expert' and knew that that was not the case. The only facilities are toilets at each end of the carriage with a wash basin. Any washing of the person, the presenters explained, has to be with wet wipes. The man was very unimpressed and his body language showed it. Someone asked whether Perm was worth a visit to which the answer was 'I wouldn't bother'. That made me feel sorry for Perm! I asked my own naïve question, for some reason focusing on whether AA batteries - for my camera - were readily available in Russia and, with a smile from the JGR staff, was humoured with the answer 'of course'. However, from that I took away the knowledge that shops there would have roughly the same day-to-day items on their shelves as shops here including the wet wipes and AA batteries! Overall, it was a really good informative evening that made me want to go to Russia there and then and I left enthused and with a much, much greater understanding as to what was and was not realistic in terms of where to visit.

I decided to look more fully at JGR. They offered several different group trips including into Mongolia and China as well as between Moscow and Vladivostok. The one I decided would best suite me took place in June 2011, a month which the Lonely Planet and Bryn Thomas books said was good for travel in Russia, lasted for thirteen days and started in Moscow, known for its Kremlin, St Basil's Cathedral and GUM store, with a stopover at Ekaterinberg, where the last Czar, also spelt Tsar, and his family were murdered, another stop at the city of Irkutsk with Lake Baikal nearby, and finishing at Vladivostok, the home of the Russian Pacific Fleet. The itinerary was set down clearly on the JGR website.

I pondered for a couple of weeks. I put together a rough budget. I got a cost from Real Russia for the train journeys only and compared this with the total JGR price. I checked out JGR again and noted that they were based towards Heathrow Airport and therefore within physical reach as well as by e-mail and telephone, even though they are an online company. I further noted that they were ATOL protected, would book flights and handle my visa application and had a website which I found clearer than their competitors. With some hesitation I went to my PC, took a deep breath, in fact several deep breaths, and booked. It was a click here, a click there, a deposit paid by card and that was it. In fact it was so easy it was a bit of an anti-climax, compensated for by the exhilaration and thrill of the decision I had made. After all the planning I would, at last, in June 2011, be spending thirteen days in lands far, far away!

Now attention had to be given to some practicalities. The next day I booked the time in June off work, having already checked office diaries to make sure there would be no issues with staff coverage. I telephoned around for travel insurance but eventually took that out through JGR as well, declaring and excluding my pre-existing but under-control anxiety issues. Having done that I was able to live the next few days in a state of extreme excitement tempered with extreme fear at what I was intending. Was this a wise thing to do? Was this a step too far out of my comfort zone for me as a first-time traveller? Were my nerves sufficiently strong? What if I didn't like it? What if I got lost? What if JGR were not as reliable as they seemed? Just what point was I trying to prove to myself?

To help deal with these doubts I wanted to keep my venture quiet from friends and family, just as a way of giving me less pressure, less well-intentioned but unhelpful curious questioning and to give more space for dealing with my anxieties. I felt it was much better to return successful than to leave with the burden of others' expectations. However, there was no chance of that. The dates for my adventure clashed with a family celebration and I had to explain why I couldn't attend and so the news leaked out. Fortunately, no one said 'don't go'.

Departure wouldn't be for five months or so and that gave time for more visits to my local library and more reading since my knowledge so far was mostly only what I had learned from the Bryn Thomas and Lonely Planet books.

I started the visa process with JGR. This was straight forward, needing payment of their fee and application costs, completion of an online form sent by JGR, returned to them, corrected by them and then sent back with strict instructions to do nothing other than print off, sign, attach photographs and send to them with my passport. The form itself was very long and the questions very intrusive, wanting to know my employment, education and family details, all to make sure that I wasn't a spy or crook. However, that is Russian bureaucracy for you. I could have arranged delivery by courier but, being untrusting and wanting to know exactly where JGR's office was, I sat for an hour on a noisy and rattling train on London Underground's Piccadilly Line heading out of central London. I got off at the right station, found the right building, an anonymous office block, and was buzzed inside by the entryphone system. Then I waited patiently in the ground floor reception area until a young Russian lady arrived from the upper floors and I handed over the documents. When I asked for a receipt for my passport she smiled, reassured me that they wouldn't steal it - in effect a verbal pat on the head - and I was won over. I walked away without a receipt but trusting and the lady was right - they didn't steal my passport and a couple of weeks later JGR sent me a message to collect the passport with its visa now entered.

Once I had made full payment when requested by JGR they e-mailed my flight details with Aeroflot to me together with a seven-page list of joining instructions. These gave each hotel, the tour programme for each city, transfer instructions, with confirmation that this would be by drivers holding JGR sign boards, train times and numbers, which I was able to double check in part online, all of this set out day by day. Additionally, there was more general information about Russia such as currency, health risks, a contact telephone number for JGR from within Russia in case of emergency and a short 'what to bring' list and document check list as well as some practical advice. By e-mail I raised a few queries on the itinerary which were satisfactorily answered and that was it. For everything else I would need to trust their arrangements.

Alongside these processes I visited Stanford Map Shop in central London - the advantage of living in the capital - and bought off the shelf a map for the whole of Russia which showed the railway lines, together with a map of central Moscow and, not being on the shelf, ordered maps in Cyrillic - all that were available - for Ekaterinberg, Irkutsk and Vladivostok. These took a few weeks to arrive but did so in plenty of time. Also, I printed off the internet an A4 map showing the time zones in Russia and an A4 map of Listvyanka where I would be staying on the shore of Lake Baikal. This need for maps was driven by my insecurities but when it came to it the most useful were the map of the whole of Russia, so I could plot the train's progress, and that for central Moscow.

Despite my fear of needles I plucked up my courage and booked an appointment with my GP practice. Looking away as various injections were administered I was duly inoculated against tetanus, diphtheria, polio and hepatitis A among others, some of these being boosters and all free in 2011 but chargeable now. I made sure I had the required supply of my prescription medications.

The internet gave me some idea of the rouble exchange rate but nevertheless I walked through the foreign currency outlets in my nearby main high street and finally ordered an amount of roubles in brightly coloured notes of various denominations from Eurochange. I obtained a travel card from a travel agent's bureaux de change and loaded this with £250 sterling as my emergency money.

In the same high street I stocked up on the clothes I thought I would need, principally from Primark. Primark was useful since I had come to the view that I would not try to wash my clothes as I travelled but would simply throw them away once they were at the end of their 'wear' time and before they became smelly! Therefore, low cost, even if low quality, items were very appropriate for most garments especially underwear and T-shirts. However, I did go for better quality trousers since I would only be taking one pair and failure in these would prove difficult as well as embarrassing. A visit to Sainsbury's stocked me with a suitable array of powdered soups, pot noodle packets, according to JGR these being the train traveller's staple diet, and some biscuits, AA batteries, wet wipes, Paracetamol and a few treats. I obtained a second memory card for my camera. Finally, I added credit to my old but very reliable pay-as-you-go mobile flip 'phone, the only mobile 'phone I had.

With the taxi to Heathrow Airport booked for 5.30am on the day of departure, which I reckoned would give plenty of time to catch the 10.35am flight, and which I then double checked the day before, all I had to do was pack, repack and repack yet again!

And I repacked even more than that. Since I would be having to carry my luggage for the whole journey I decided to go hand luggage only. Therefore, every inch of space was valuable and used. I allowed the weather forecast to guide me and so did not pack any cold weather clothes, deciding that I would layer up if the climate chilled, which I was to find it did in the evenings. I took no heavy waterproof coat but only an umbrella and a plastic pack-a-mac. As well as the Bryn Thomas book I took a handful of fiction books to read, choosing thin books with smaller print which I would leave behind once I had read them. I did not take the Lonely Planet book nor did I take Tolstoy's War and Peace - at JGRs evening presentation they had told us they knew of only one person who had read all of that on the journey! I looked out my travel kettle element and a mug. My money I put in envelopes and spread them around my luggage and the gilet I intended to wear to reduce the risk of losing it all or having it all stolen. I put aside my UK money for the journey home as well as my London Oyster travel card. I found a spare tin opener. I made up a first aid kit. I made sure that my padlock worked and packed a chain. I got a notebook. I looked out three watches - one for GMT, one for local time and one for Moscow time, this last being the time on which Russian trains run. A squash ball was squeezed in to use as a wash basin plug. I wanted to take a mascot so looked out a small, soft toy Tigger which I actually kept concealed from others for the whole trip - after all, should an adult be needing a soft toy? - and then, to the horror of my family, I tied onto the top of my packed bag my ukulele, the playing of which is my other manifestation of a mid-life crisis!

Eventually I was able to get my luggage into a standard soft hand luggage bag, topped with my ukulele with the spare space in the instrument bag filled with socks, and also into a drawstring bag. I kept electrical items accessible for ease at airport security. I filled all the pockets of my gilet and filled a belt bag. These - the gilet and belt bag - would be worn the whole time and not leave my side except when asleep in locked hotel rooms. My passport and paperwork I kept handy with copies in my luggage bag. I certainly cannot travel now with such an amount as hand luggage. Finally, in a carrier bag, I had a couple of pastries to eat in the waiting time after I had got through Heathrow Airport security.

The night before departure I lined up all my things by the front door and got an early night although a mixture of nervousness and excited anticipation meant I slept only fitfully. The next morning, Sunday 12 June 2011, I was up early, had a good breakfast and rechecked everything ready for the taximan's ring at the door. The ring from the taximan came dead on time and so, leaving small gifts of jewellery on the breakfast table for my wife and daughter to find later as a thank you for letting me go, and having proved to the taximan that I did have my passport and had not forgotten that - he must have had some bad experiences with people forgetting and having to be taken back home to collect - I said goodbye to home, jumped into the taxi and was off.

I was on my way to Russia!

ARRIVAL

MY HEATHROW AIRPORT EXPERIENCE was good. The taxi driver went around London's orbital motorway, the M25, without any hold-ups and after pulling into the airport's Terminal Two roadway at around 6.45am I paid him and taking my luggage followed the signs, went inside and approached the Aeroflot desk. My electronic ticket was exchanged for a boarding pass, I went through security without any difficulties, got my bearings, worked out the location of the different boarding gates, checked the departure boards and then headed for a coffee shop and settled down with a latte and the pastries I had brought with me. Hunger satisfied I bought a couple of bottles of water in readiness for arrival in Moscow where the tap water, not only there but throughout Russia, is not to be drunk or indeed go anywhere near one's mouth. All drinking water has to be bought in unopened plastic bottles. I then idled the time away watching other passengers coming and going, with the airport being busy but not uncomfortably so.

At about half past nine the relevant gate number appeared on the display screen and I made my way with other passengers to the next area of seating outside the boarding gantry. Forty-five minutes or so before departure time the boarding process commenced. I stowed my bags in the overhead locker and took my allocated aisle seat, keeping my fragile ukulele on my lap. I was pleased to note that the aeroplane was a modern Airbus A320 and so hopefully not as prone to fall out of the sky as folklore historically said happened to Aeroflot planes. As we got ready for take-off and the doors were shut and the emergency procedure 'dance' performed by the Aeroflot stewards I wondered whether anyone else on the flight would be on the JGR tour. Looking around I saw no likely candidates.

I read a bit on the flight and had a picture conversation with the man next to me. He was Russian and didn't speak English but was able to tell me with pen and paper that he was a tourist, had been in the United Kingdom for the last two weeks and had seen Buckingham Palace, Tower Bridge, St Paul's Cathedral and somewhere else which made sense at the time but the drawing of which I have no chance of interpreting now. Also, he drew a picture of a typical Russian timber house which was to prove remarkably accurate. Now he was returning to his home to the north of Moscow. In turn I explained to him that I was travelling from Moscow to Vladivostok on the train. For speaking only through pen and paper I thought we had had a good chat.

Poor but edible food was served, landing cards were distributed to those non-Russians who needed them, which included me, to be surrendered on departure from Russia, and after a smooth and uneventful flight we came in to land, on time, at half past five Moscow time, at Sheremetyevo Airport. I shut my eyes and gripped the arm rests until the aeroplane had stopped bumping on the runway. When we were safely down the plane erupted with clapping which made me wonder whether the flight was somehow more precarious than I knew! However, I had finally arrived in Moscow, the capital of Russia, in the land that Winston Churchill famously described as 'a riddle, wrapped in a mystery, inside an enigma'.

The origins of present-day Russia are unclear. The kingdom of the Rus was founded in the year 988 in Kiev, with the Rus being of Viking descent, although some will point to the foundation of Novgorod in the year 859 as a candidate for that nation's birth. Marriage links were made with the Byzantine Empire from which modern day Russia takes its Orthodox religion, it's double headed eagle emblem and its claim that Moscow is the third Rome after Rome itself, which fell to the barbarians in 476AD, and then after the capital of the eastern Roman Empire, Constantinople, later called Byzantium, which fell to the Ottomans in 1453. In time the sovereigns took the title Czar as in Caesar, also written as Tsar. Before the twelfth century the Kievan kingdom had split into separate principalities with the main ones being based on Kiev and on Yaroslavl, a city north-east of Moscow. Then came the Mongols, destroying all in their path and for three hundred years subjugating the whole area.

Therefore, the history of the real modern Russia starts in the late fifteenth century with the rise of the principality of Muscovy, Moscow, the throwing off of the Mongols and the expansion of its territory to the river Volga. In the seventeenth century Muscovy expanded east of the Ural Mountains, taking only sixty years for its dominion to reach the Pacific Ocean and then into Alaska. Peter the Great, in the early eighteenth century, forcibly recreated Muscovy as a European nation, leaving behind its Asian character and gaining territory from Sweden around the Baltic Sea and moving the capital to the new city of St Petersburg. It was now that the name 'Muscovy' fell out of use and came to be replaced by 'Russia'. Catherine the Great, in the middle of the eighteenth century, expanded what had become the Russian Empire southwards to the Black Sea, pushing the Ottomans out of southern Ukraine, including the Crimea, and pushing westwards into Poland. In 1867, under Czar Alexander II, Alaska was sold to the USA. His son, Alexander III, ordered the construction of the Trans-Siberian Railway which took place between 1891 and 1904. Russia's more recent history is better known - the disastrous Russo-Japanese War of 1904-5, which would have been even more disastrous for Russia without the Trans-Siberian Railway, the failed 1905 revolution, the First World War, the 1917 revolutions followed by civil war, the founding of the USSR with its capital moved back to Moscow, the Great Patriotic War, what we know as the Second World War, with its huge casualties and destruction, and in 1991 the falling apart of the USSR into its constituent republics. And here I was, on Sunday 12th June 2011, in this ancient and historic land.

With no hold luggage to collect I was able to exit through border control and the customs' green channel fairly quickly, aided by signage with English written beneath the Russian Cyrillic script. Immediately on the public side of the exit I was faced with a barrage of offers from a crowd of taxi drivers wanting my business. I waved a gentle declining hand at all of them, looked for someone holding a JGR sign and not finding anyone I walked away from the crowd and leant discretely against a column and waited, holding down some apprehension. I was here in Russia, the country of my dreams, pushing my boundaries to, for me, the extreme. I wondered what I would do if no one appeared with a JGR sign. Would my adventure end at an airport? The wait was long and the arrivals hall was emptying when a man with a JGR board walked in. As I quickly joined him two other people, who I hadn't spotted and must have had their own discrete columns to lean against, joined him as well.

As we introduced ourselves the first, June from Swindon, said she was glad there were others on the trip since she hadn't been given any indication of numbers. She had been to Russia before as had the other, Howard, who came from Kent but worked in the City of London and knew there would be two or three others on the journey. I was relieved to meet them both since the possibility of being left to do the trip solo had never even occurred to me and would have given me a complete meltdown!

Outside in the heat of the Russian summer our bags and cases were loaded into the people carrier taxi and off we went into central Moscow, along roads lined with nine storey blocks of flats, in what seemed to be an anarchic race with other vehicles and with no rules. Somehow we arrived safely at the large and modern Katerina Hotel on the south bank of the Moskva River. We thanked the driver, gathered our bags, booked in, had our passports copied and took the lift up to our rooms, arranging to meet up again in an hour's time after we had all freshened up.

That short time later, suitably refreshed and with my map in my hand we all headed out of the hotel and started exploring the city before us, strolling up to Gorky Park with its white classical entrance and lawns, flowers beds and fountains. Having to some extent mastered the art of looking left right left when crossing roads, against a lifetime of training to do the opposite, we strolled in the hot weather past the Peter the Great statue, over the footbridge across the river and towards the Cathedral of Christ the Saviour, a 1990s reconstruction of the original mid-nineteenth century building which was blown up by the communists and replaced with a swimming pool. A year later this cathedral was to become the venue for the gig which brought the punk rock band Pussy Riot to prominence. From the bridge we viewed the Kremlin. We admired its star topped towers, huge red walls and rising behind them the elegant eighteenth century palace buildings and older white painted churches with golden domed towers before walking past those red walls, with a section of timber scaffolding and hoarding guarded by a ring of soldiers in parade uniform and with big caps. We never did discover what secret building work was going on. I remembered that someone once said to me that the size of the cap can be indicative of the size of the dictatorship and I concluded on that basis that the dictatorship in Russia must be large. Eventually we found ourselves in Red Square with its GUM store, the red granite clad Lenin mausoleum with its guards and queue of visitors and the multi-towered St Basil's Cathedral with its many domes looking like coloured ice cream cones. We walked past the small and rebuilt Kazan Cathedral, the rebuilt Resurrection Gate, both buildings previously demolished by the communists to allow them to more easily parade their troops and tanks in Red Square. Having viewed the guarded Tomb of the Unknown Warrior and the eternal flame memorial we eventually found our way back to the hotel, observing the rumbling electric trams and smoother electric trolley buses as we went, both a novelty for me, and then we relaxed in the hotel restaurant with a light meal, which for me was an omelette. On paying I discovered that a thousand rouble note was not easy to exchange. However, I learned that hotels are generally a good place to eat. We checked our schedules ready for tomorrow and then departed to our own rooms for sleep, not that that came easily with the change in time zones, party noise from somewhere below and realising that I missed listening to the BBC on a radio! A text message conversation home and a soft ukulele strum helped me to relax and drift off.

The next day, Monday, started and continued bright and sunny. Once showered and dressed I rechecked the tour itinerary, noting that a tour guide would be meeting us in the hotel lobby at 10am, and then wandered down to the ground floor, found the restaurant, showed the room number on my key when asked by the supervisor and, with no sign of the others yet, enjoyed a really good cooked breakfast plus fruit, pastry and coffee. Finished and with time to spare and the others presumably still emerging from their slumbers, I went outside to look at the nearby monastery, visible through my room window and whose bells had serenaded me as I awoke. The monastery, which I later found out was the Novospassky Monastery, had white painted walls with conical hatted towers and a huge baroque bell tower entrance way. However, there was no public access to see the five-domed church inside.

Returning to the hotel room I grabbed my courtesy water bottles, packed my bag and booked out, leaving the bag padlocked and chained in the hotel store room. I joined June and Howard waiting in the lobby and shortly after and on time our guide for the day's tour of Moscow arrived. She introduced herself as Helen and started walking us around the city sights, giving good and clear explanations in excellent English and first of all taking us into the Metro, a must-see attraction with its magnificent mosaics in the well-designed and elegant stations, particularly Komsomolskaya, Ploshchad Revolyutsii, Mayakovskaya and Dostoyevskaya stations. After an hour or so we came out of the Metro to view the Bolshoi Ballet building and then, tiring, into Red Square, a UNESCO World Heritage Site and the scene of many concerts as well, as already said, of military parades and with its Lenin Mausoleum and the GUM store with its atrium and glazed roof and upmarket stores. There we offered Helen a coffee break but she explained that, whilst it was up to us, there was a lot yet to see. So we allowed her to move us on without stopping and with some amount of smug satisfaction on our part she took us past a long queue through the Kremlin's Kutafya Tower and main Trinity Gate Tower and straight into that citadel.

The Kremlin is worth a whole day on its own but we did a reduced yet very satisfactory and acceptable tour of the grounds and the main ecclesiastical buildings, the fifteenth century Assumption and Annunciation Cathedrals, with Helen explaining the history of the eighty one meter high Ivan the Great Bell Tower, the Czar bell and cannon, but leaving for some future return visit other areas including the eighteenth century palaces and late 1950s State Kremlin Palace and the Armoury building with its Faberge collection. Helen carried a spare headscarf for June when we went into the churches - the respectful rule is heads covered for women and shoulders and knees covered for both genders. Helen's commentary was very good and she explained that she had learned her English from BBC programmes! However, she did stumble in one church in the Kremlin where she described the dove of the Holy Spirit on a wall painting as a pigeon. It politely amused me but when she asked us if that was right we told her the proper bird name. One noticeable behaviour was the way she crossed herself in churches, as we found all Russians instinctively do, even though she said she wasn't very religious. It was fascinating to find out more of the life of an average Russian citizen. We sympathised with our similarity of concerns, with Helen explaining the difficulties of very expensive but neglected housing where she lived in southern Moscow and which was the product of capitalism and not the previous communism. Also, she commented that we were visiting at a good time with the temperature only 30C since last summer it had reached 40C with pollution as well.

Helen walked us back to the hotel in good time and we said our thanks and goodbyes. As we double checked our itinerary we grabbed a drink from the reception facilities, retrieved our luggage and were all ready for the taxi which turned up on time at 3pm and took us to Moscow's Kazansky train station. Moscow's train stations are usefully named by their destinations so, for example, Belorussky station serves Belarus, Kursky station serves Kursk and so on. The train we were to catch at Kazansky station would take us through Kazan. The taxi dropped us off outside the station for the 4.50pm train and with excitement we realised that this, at last, would be the start of our long, long journey eastwards into the very wildernesses of Siberia!

INTO THE URALS

HOWARD, JUNE AND I stood on the concourse of Kazansky station with time to spare and looked on at the bustling crowd around us as we got our bearings. We gazed at the electronic information board trying to work out which column was arrivals and which was departures. Eventually we were able to marry this up with our itinerary information which for me said, with that for the others being similar, 'Departure to Yekaterinburg. Train No. 0166A. Carriage 05. Berth 02. Ticket Delivery - Electronic Check-In. Please go directly to your train and board the carriage using your passport. No paper tickets required. Ticket reservation reference 762603 40700021.' The information boards eventually gave the train number, destination and departure time expected alongside a platform number.

Still having time to spare we got ourselves a coffee from one of the concourse kiosks before we headed to the train, the outside of which was a smart two-tone grey with red trimmings and which was clean, without any graffiti or dirt. The very smartly dressed lady attendant of carriage number 5, the provodnitsa, - if there had been a male attendant he would be a provodnik but they were not to feature on our journey - checked our passports before letting us board and then remained guarding the carriage door. It was noticeable that at every station stop along the way the provodnitsas did the same. They disembarked and each stood on guard by the door until the train was ready to leave whereupon they would return onboard, raise the steps set within the doorway and secure the door.

We wandered down the carriage corridor and found our four-berth compartment with its red upholstered bench seats, used later as beds, and two red drop-down bunks, a table with box safe beneath and high level and below seat storage areas, TV screen and a Russian fellow traveller. We were in a top of the range corridor train pulled by a massive engine powered from overhead electric lines but nevertheless were struck by how hot it was inside. Fortunately, the air conditioning kicked in once the train was moving.

There was no mutual language between us and our Russian travelling companion but communicating our greetings with handshakes and using hand signals we exchanged names. Vladimir accepted the presence of three strange foreigners very well and in our own way we all conversed together.

As the train got moving we settled in and gazed out of the windows at the scruffy Moscow suburbs with tower blocks of flats in the distance. This view gradually changed into mile after mile and hour after hour of birch forest. Within the train the corridor with its samovar became a communal meeting place.

We discovered that one of the joys of travelling on the regular long distance commuter trains was meeting real Russians, something a fully escorted tour would not give in the same way. Our friendly companion Vladimir was a retired engineer, had been visiting Moscow to celebrate his brother's sixtieth birthday and was now returning to his house in a small village or town somewhere in the Urals.

Other travellers were equally friendly. Some were lone travellers on business, others were families. Football was always a good subject that bridged our limited language skills, with the Russians having an intimate knowledge of the English Premier League. These conversations passed the time and, thankfully, our fellow passengers smiled at the sound of my quiet and soft ukulele playing. We studied the timetable fixed up in the corridor and managed to work out the different columns telling us, all in Moscow time, when the train would stop and for how long, although whenever it did stop we always checked for how long with the provodnitsa. Getting left behind on a station platform would be disastrous!

Brightly coloured and clean local stations, a number with tall, elegant nineteenth century Czarist water towers and memorial steam engines painted black with a red star at the front, and villages with wooden houses with corrugated roofs, as well as huge anonymous rivers and wide grasslands, passed by outside. Inside we investigated the other carriages, those with two-berth cabins and the dormitory carriages at the very end.

We found the restaurant car and managed to successfully order from a menu with slightly strange English translation and enjoyed a reasonable meal. We chatted together and got to know each other more with June revealing that she worked for a small print company. Howard and I found that we came from the same area of London and had attended nearby schools, although not in the same school year.

As night fell we readied for sleep, pulling down the top bunks, one of which was mine, and changing in the wc. These wcs, one at each end of every carriage, were kept impeccably clean by the provodnitsas and not abused by anyone. They had the essentials including a hose for hair washing and showering, with water dispersing across the grated floor, which therefore was always wet. I realised how useful a pair of flip flops would be if I had them and a decent bag to hang off the hook on the door in which to keep clothes.

Returning to the compartment I undid the sealed polythene bag containing a blanket, sheets and pillow case and made up my drop down bed. As I settled down, peeping through the edge of the rolled down window blind, the wonders of modern communication meant that the text messages I sent home were answered immediately.

My night's sleep was not good. It was cold and sharing a bed with some of my luggage made everything a bit cramped. I realised that occupying a bed on a train was very different to occupying a spacious hotel room and also I needed to keep a torch and alarm clock handy without dropping them over the edge. However, the gentle rocking motion of the train was soothing and I realised that the idea of the Trans-Siberian Express is fiction - it is not an express but does move steadily and relentlessly on at a speed, I would suppose, of 40 to 50 miles per hour. I was aware of many goods trains passing and watched them through the gap around the window blind. As I did a toilet trip in the early hours, achieved without waking up anyone else, I was surprised to find a different provodnitsa in full uniform working away cleaning the corridor areas.

At dawn the next day, Tuesday, which was at about 4am, I was woken accidentally by June moving around. Together we went to the corridor window and watched the sun rise and we both became absolutely awestruck as it glinted and beamed off the golden domes of the churches of Kazan in a very short but nevertheless very spectacular light show which words are inadequate to describe. For us this became a highlight of the trip.

Suddenly the light show was over and as the train pulled into Kazan station with its bilingual signs - in Russian and Tatar - for a fifteen minute stop June and I slipped clothes over our pyjamas, left the others sleeping and went out onto the platform to buy breakfast at one of the kiosks. A few other passengers had the same idea. My purchase was a crispy honey roll and a cheese filled pastry which I took back to the train to eat at a proper breakfast hour. The other essential to buy was bottled water although I trusted that the boiled water from the samovar was safe.

As the day progressed passengers relaxed and sat around talking, reading, playing games at the compartment tables or otherwise stayed in bed dozing. I found that I needed to keep a routine and structure to my time so started the day proper by washing my hair and dressing in the wc, without getting my clothes wet from the floor, which was not easy, and then enjoying my newly bought breakfast from Kazan. The day I spent as others did, reading, talking and studying the scenery out of the window. For long stretches all that was visible was forest, tree after tree after tree. Elsewhere the number of abandoned buildings was noticeable and it seems, with its huge land space, that abandonment, rather than demolition and reusing the site, is acceptable, with rebuilding carried out on a fresh site. There were many one and two storey timber houses with brightly painted window shutters and lattice carvings to the roof verges and this style of building did not change along the whole length of the journey, all the way to Vladivostok.

Russians are generous and at one station stop Vladimir bought two dried herrings, a popular food, from one of the platform vendors who were present at all of the larger stations with their wares spread out on the platform, some on ground sheets and under sun umbrellas. As the train moved on Vladimir shared the herrings with us together with a bottle of vodka with a chilli at the bottom. It was very kind of him but I am tee-total, as I had to explain with no Russian language skills and without giving offence! Also, I was very suspicious of some platform food, not wanting food poisoning, and June was equally hesitant, so we left Howard to pick up the challenge which he bravely did. However, I did let a very small piece of herring pass my lips, just to show willing.

As the day went on and a snack lunch was had my stomach did start to play up a bit, not I think in anyway associated with the herring, but I realised that my diet needed to stabilise if I was to cope for the whole trip and so resolved that fruit and at least one decent meal a day would be essential.

Vladimir left us at a small station somewhere along the route and we said our goodbyes and gave him a wave through the window as the train moved on. Forests continued with some burned areas indicative of forest fires. We realised that we were going through country which was becoming more hilly and that this must be the Ural Mountains, although there was not a mountain in sight. Many goods trains full of quarried stone passed before it was time to put our used bedding into a pile at the end of the corridor and gather our possessions ready for arrival at 8.14pm at Ekaterinberg, an arrival which was timed to the minute although slightly engineered since we came to note that trains would wait outside a station rather than arrive early!

Ekaterinberg - as already said the anglicised spelling is Yekaterinburg - was founded in 1723 and named after Catherine

I, the wife of Peter the Great. It was on the historic Siberian highway, little more than a mud track, and prospered due to mining and its iron works. It is the place where the last Czar and his family were murdered and in communist times was called Sverdlovsk and was a closed city with no foreigners allowed. It is currently one of the largest cities in Russia.

As we disembarked from the train we were glad to see a man on the platform with a board with our names waiting to take us to our Ekaterinberg hotel. The taxi took us through town, past a mix of Soviet concrete, Czarist timber and glass-clad modern buildings and dropped us off at the Guru Hotel, slightly away from the city centre and on the second floor of a 1980s building with a restaurant and leisure centre beneath. There the receptionist photocopied our passports and handed over keys for us to find our rooms.

The first thing any Trans-Siberian traveller does on breaking their journey and finding a hotel room is to have a shower and freshen up. Having allowed a suitable time for each of us to do that we joined together again and wandered into the city centre on the other side of the river Iset, around which Ekaterinberg was founded, viewing the red spiked monument in the middle of the bridge on our way, before returning and enjoying a meal with a chicken main course in the restaurant part of the hotel. Then we went to our rooms and crashed out. I'm not sure about the others but I slept very soundly.

The next morning, Wednesday, I showered again, because I could, secured all my belongings and padlocked my bag to the bed out of sight of the door. I met the others for a Danish-style breakfast. After breakfast we decided to find a supermarket to buy provisions since our common view was that the food in the train restaurant car was not adequate on its own. We passed by some interesting and pleasant buildings before finding the shop and then had to decipher the labels on what we were buying. I bought some tins of fruit and some biscuits, enough for the next two day's train journey, but not too much since everything I bought I would have to carry. I was feeling a little under the weather but made it back to the hotel and felt better by the time we were due to meet our tour guide at ten o'clock in the hotel reception.

We had to check out of our rooms so left our luggage at the hotel reception. We weren't happy with the security since our bags were only put around a corner rather than into a locked store so I produced my padlock and chain again and we bound them to each other and to some furniture, out of sight of the hotel entrance.

Our tour guide, Olga, turned up on time but there was some confusion since she had expected to meet a lady with a young child. While she spent several minutes on her mobile 'phone clarifying this with her employers we speculated as to which of Howard and I was the young child. Eventually we nominated Howard for that role!

We set off with Olga in her hired people carrier taxi with driver and she took us on a city tour to the statues of Vasily Nikitich Tatishchev and Vilim Ivanovich de Gennin, the city founders, located by the river, to a pair of large joined nineteenth century houses, one very plain and one richly ornamented which reflected the different lifestyles of the two brothers who each owned one of them, and then to the large Church Upon The Blood built after the fall of the Soviet Union next to the site of the demolished Ipatiev House where the Czar and his family were murdered in 1918. Outside there is an evocative sculpture of the Czar and his family descending to the basement of the house to their deaths. A smaller Old Believers' chapel is on the actual house site.

As we went Olga shared some of her life story. She had spent three months in Manchester in the late 1990s as part of her English language training and is now a teacher acting as a freelance tour guide in the three month school summer holiday. She lived in a flat by the Iset river but has a country house, a dacha, about seventy kilometers away, as have a large number of Russians so they can grow vegetables. Dachas and vegetable growing were promoted by the communists to ease food shortages. However, all she grows are herbs and flowers. She could not understand why we were staying in the Guru Hotel rather than somewhere smarter although it seemed perfectly acceptable to us. Apparently the football stadium opposite the hotel was due to be used for the 2018 Football World Cup.

After the city tour the taxi took us on a fairly long journey to Ganina Yama about sixteen kilometers north of Ekaterinberg. This is a post-USSR complex of seven chapels, together called the Monastery of the Holy Martyrs and was built by the Orthodox church, with some building continuing, on the site where the bodies of the last Czar and his family were found, having been dumped down redundant pit shafts. Again, head scarves were required for ladies with shoulders and knees covered. There were some Old Believers visiting at the same time as us with the ladies having the whole of their arms covered and skirts down to the ground. The monastery complex had its own guide to show visitors around so the very competent Olga could relax. It was here that I first encountered filthy squat hole-in-the-ground toilets and definitely did not use them for any of my functions, deciding that these were something to be completely avoided!

Next it was on to the Europe-Asia border monument about seventeen kilometers west of the city and one of several such monuments around the area. We took the required photographs of a foot each side of the border line and then jumped back into the taxi.

The taxi driver returned us to the hotel at about three o'clock and then Olga took us on a trolley bus into the city centre. Before she left us, making sure we knew the trolley bus stop we needed to find our way back to the hotel, she showed June a bookshop that June wanted to visit and Howard a shop where he could buy a new camera battery since his had failed. However, sadly, when it came to it, the camera shop couldn't find the correct battery and Howard had to buy a whole new camera.

Now on our own June took us around the area looking at some of the constructionist architecture for which Ekaterinberg is renowned. Constructionist architecture looks like its function so, for example, the tractor manufacturer's building was shaped in the form of a tractor. Also, we looked at a building with the plan shape of a hammer and sickle, although from the street it was hard to appreciate the symbolic design.

Russians are friendly. We stayed in the pedestrianised city centre and went to a Pizza Mia to eat. A group of youngsters approached us, having eyed us up as Americans. We quickly corrected them. They wanted to talk more with us but Howard felt, wisely, that we had had sufficient engagement. After eating our pizzas and moving on we were stopped in the street by a young man in green army uniform who again asked if we were American and again, we explained 'no'. Apparently he had travelled and worked in America for a few months and was now half-way through his one year of compulsory national service. We separated from him and, admiring the full-size street art statues, decided to walk a route through the city back to the hotel rather than take the trolley bus, passing the local prison and noticing an increased number of old Lada cars compared to Moscow. Later we went to the supermarket again, with the same girl on the tills - a shift of probably twelve hours - and then retrieved our luggage and waited for JGRs pre-booked taxi to arrive at 9.30pm to take us to the train station.

We checked our itinerary:

'22:50 Departure to Irkutsk. Train No 350YA Carriage: 06, Berth 018. Second Class. Ticket delivery - Train ticket vouchers. Please collect tickets at the station, ref 78030368898364. No boarding allowed without paper ticket being issued at the station'.

We looked out our vouchers and were ready.

The trip so far had been relaxed and gone smoothly which was a real fillip for my confidence. However, that now changed. The taxi arrived at the arranged time, 9.30pm, and drove through busy traffic to drop us at the train station at 10pm with the train due to depart at 10.50pm. We had plenty of time and didn't need to rush.

As soon as we walked into the train station we knew that we were in trouble and stress levels for all of us escalated out of sight.

The high-ceilinged booking hall had ten or more ticket windows, all of which were manned. In front of each were queues of at least fifteen people. The queues were hardly moving and there was the babble of loud conversation echoing around the room. Checking our watches we realised that we had only fifty minutes to queue and get our paper tickets before we had to be on the train leaving the station. Would we have enough time? Howard joined a queue in the middle of the hall and June a queue at the near end while I stayed guarding our luggage nearby. After twenty minutes of no movement at all every one of my doubts, fears and anxieties about travel suddenly returned. What would happen if we missed the train, as seemed very likely? Would we be stranded? Would we be on the streets for the night? How would we complete the rest of the journey and within our visa time? As those thoughts went through my mind I became aware of June shouting to me above the general hubbub 'This is no good. You've got to do something.' No pressure on me then!

At that moment an important official-looking black uniformed and grey haired lady came down a flight of steps next to the booking hall. June took over watching the luggage while I rushed up the steps and accosted the official saying pleadingly 'Angliski?' but no, she didn't speak English. With a bit of gesticulation at the train time on my voucher and then at the chaotic booking hall and then at my watch the penny finally dropped with her. She turned around and motioning me to follow her headed back up the steps, through long corridors and halls and eventually came to an office window. I stayed at the window and she went into the office. There followed lots of jabbering and discussion in Russian, an examination of my passport, me holding up three fingers to show I was travelling with others, and then suddenly I was put in the care of a young uniformed lad with gestures to follow him. With calls over my shoulder of 'spasiba' I kept right behind him through the halls and corridors and back down the steps at which point he went straight to the front of the nearest queue. Still on the steps I called out to June to get Howard while I watched the luggage and they both joined the youngster at the counter. Howard got his ticket and replaced me guarding the luggage but June could not get hers and couldn't understand what additional information the ticket clerk wanted. As I stood next to her at the ticket window the Russian man at the head of the queue tapped my arm and took me over to Howard who was holding some of our papers. I can't remember exactly which papers but immediately I knew that these were needed by the ticket clerk so I grabbed them and gave them to June. The rest of the process was quickly concluded, tickets issued and with 'spasibas' given again, this time to the ticket clerk and the Russian man we had queue jumped, we ran for our train and arrived out of breath at the carriage door with ten minutes to spare - all thanks to the kindness of a Russian official and a Russian man who had been pushed down the queue by us.

When I returned home I recounted this incident to JGR - after all we had had over six hours from Olga concluding our tour until the time the taxi arrived at the hotel to take us to the station and this would have been plenty of time to pick up our tickets - and they changed their system to allow tickets to be printed off in Moscow and not at separate stages of the journey.

As we breathed sighs of relief my confidence soared from rock bottom up to the stars. If I could function in a crisis like that then I should be able to deal with anything!

SIBERIA

THE TRAIN WE WERE on, now leaving Ekaterinberg, was definitely down market compared to our first train. The uniforms of the provodnitsas were not as smart, although the provodnitsas were just as hard working. There was no shower in the wcs and the toilets discharged onto the track with the cubicle locked approaching station stops and until after leaving to keep the station area clean. The railway track could be seen through the footplates separating the carriages, decorative finishes were older and there were no television screens in the compartments which had brown plastic rather that fabric upholstery.

Howard was put in a separate four-berth compartment with, as he later explained, three unsociable Russian men. June and I were with a mother and her young son, who was probably four or five years old, neither of whom spoke English although we exchanged greetings and all was friendly. Once it became dark, around midnight, and the passengers settled down to sleep, the provodnitsa locked the compartment door. We could still get out but no-one else could wander in and this was reassuring. With the Russian lady and boy in the compartment already we didn't change for bed but slept that night in our clothes. The lady and her son left in the light of the early hours at a very small village station and Howard then joined us, having slept badly with the Russians he was with getting up, or got up by the provodnitsa, and departing the train at regular intervals. We all drifted off to sleep but I was aware of a constant stream of very long goods trains passing the other way all through the night.

Getting up in the morning, Thursday, I again found it helpful to keep to a routine, especially since we would be two days on this train. I made sure I shaved and got dressed into fresh clothes rather than drifting around in yesterday's garments or night things as some other travellers did but not, I hasten to add, June and Howard. I had a hot drink in my mug, with the hot water drawn from the carriage samovar at the end of the corridor, to blow off my mental cobwebs. Next, I cleared any rubbish I found into our waste carrier bag which we considered essential to avoid living in a 'pigsty' and then, needing a bit of 'me' time, which we each needed at some point, I went to the restaurant car, looked at the menu and picked something for breakfast. This received the answer 'Nyet' from the attendant so I picked something else which wasn't available either and then sent the attendant, who was also the cook, away. The next ten minutes I spent with my phrase book and dictionary out trying to understand what was on offer. In the end I had scrambled eggs which were not on the menu but which were what was prepared for me when I asked for fried eggs. Along with a coffee I was content. I paid and then sat and read before wandering back to the compartment suitably refreshed. However, my experience confirmed what we all realised, namely that the restaurant car wasn't of much use and we were glad we had brought our own provisions on board.

Hour after successive hour the train rumbled on, June describing it as not boring but monotonous although I would describe it as relaxing. From somewhere, I know not where, June, who was full of surprises, found a quote from Chekhov's Sakhalin Island which seemed relevant to her:

'If while travelling the countryside possesses any significance at all for you then, going from Russia to Siberia you could have a very boring time from the Urals right up to the Yenisei. The chilly plain, the twisted birch trees, the pools, the occasional islands, snow in May and the barren, blank bank of the Ob - these are all that the memory succeeds in retaining from the first 2000 versts.'

I am pleased to say that that was not my experience. I read and gazed out of the window at the endless grassland of the Siberian plain stretching as far as the eye could see and then up to the Arctic. In several places the course of the railway line had been altered and upgraded, a constant process from the moment the Trans-Siberian was first built, with old redundant bridge piers present in the many rivers. I tried to learn a bit of Russian and made lists of things I would need to get such as more AA batteries for my camera, which seemed to be using a lot, and also more wet wipes.

Each time we crossed into a new time zone, as we did a couple of times this day, we broke our routines to hold a tea ceremony in celebration, indulging in a treat such as a cake or biscuit and to the bemusement of the Russian passengers. Otherwise, I kept to a strict eating routine of breakfast, lunch, afternoon snack and dinner with my lunch and dinner being a tin of fruit eaten straight from the can and once the can was empty filling it with pot noodles with hot water from the samovar and then throwing it away, so avoiding what would be the impossible task of cleaning out my cup, and all followed by biscuits for dessert.

Whenever we could we disembarked onto the platforms and on some of the longer stops, such as Omsk, we were able to have a glance outside of the station.

We examined the carriage timetable with its many columns and decided we would stay awake for the crossing of the river Ob, one of Siberia's great rivers, with its city of Novosibirsk, the third largest city in Russia, at around midnight. When we reached the Ob, just before midnight, it was dark but, contradicting Chekhov, a large number of dock cranes lined the river bank and showed against the skyline as the train rumbled over the very long river bridge. The stop in Novosibirsk would be for an hour so once in the station we asked the provodnitsa to lock our compartment door and then went onto the platform. A kind Russian man, a fellow passenger, took a photo of the three of us with each of our cameras. I titled the result 'The Three Russian Bears'! I think we were a bit of a novelty as foreigners and we may have been the only ones on the train although there was a rumour that a couple of Americans were somewhere on board.

Novosibirsk has the largest train station of the whole of the Trans-Siberian Railway so we went exploring. That was when we learned that taking photographs inside the station is not permitted with a railway official shouting across the magnificent and crowded waiting room for Howard to put his raised camera away. Confusingly the taking of photographs is allowed on the Moscow metro. We made ourselves scarce and headed outside, trying at the manned entrance barrier to ask the question 'If we go out will we be allowed back in?' Language failed us until a kind young Russian girl offered to translate for us and we were reassured that we would be allowed to re-enter the station. We headed into the large station square with its food stalls, skateboarders and crowds and we admired the illuminated green and cream station elevations.

We had no time to stray further than the station square and returned safely and on time to the train. Back on board we slept and slept so well that we missed the crossing of the Yennisei river, another of Siberia's great waterways, and its crossing city of Krasnoyarsk. As we woke up the next day, Friday, suitably refreshed we needed to alter our watches to a new time zone. My watch on Greenwich Mean Time had somehow stopped with the winding button accidentally pulled out so I had to do some careful calculations to re-set it to the right time. It seemed to start working again without any difficulty.

At one stop we were joined in our compartment by Igor, a Russian man probably in his late twenties or early thirties, travelling home to the city of Irkutsk. He worked for a Swiss chemical firm as their rep., covering all of eastern Siberia but which was probably a population of only ten million people. Again, his English was excellent. As we chatted he revealed that, because he went to university, he had been able to avoid national service. Like me he was tee-total and had given up alcohol. He explained that the well-known Russian alcohol problem was not exclusively caused by vodka but also by beer drinking. I asked whether he knew of any Baptist churches in Irkutsk since we would be there on a Sunday and if there was even half a chance I would attend one. His interesting response was to distinguish Baptist churches as Christian as opposed to Orthodox and

Catholic churches. However, he did not know of any. We shared some of our food with him and found he had never experienced fig rolls, of which I had a couple of packets still uneaten that I had brought with me from the UK. He liked them and when we eventually parted at Irkutsk I left my remaining unopened packet with him to enjoy.

As on previous occasions long goods trains continued to pass by, one carrying tanks and other military equipment and others logs. We knew we were leaving the Siberian plain as the scenery became ever more hilly and the train then started to climb and negotiate tight curves through some of the valleys on the route. While Howard had an afternoon nap June and I decided not to disturb him but just take a photograph with his camera of the length of the train with the engine visible on a bend, to make sure he didn't completely miss the moment.

That day, Friday, passed by slowly. We realised that we were getting to the end of our rations and knew that the onboard restaurant was inadequate. However, we managed to survive and went to sleep that night to the gentle rocking of the train, looking forward to our 9.36am arrival the next day, Saturday, in the city of Irkutsk.

Irkutsk was founded by Cossacks during the Russian expansion across Siberia in the seventeenth century. It was established at the confluence of the mighty Angara river and the smaller Irkut river. From 1652 it was used as a site for over-wintering with a fort built in 1661. Its position made it a centre on the trade route between Russia and China, later it became a centre for the exiles from the defeated Decembrist Revolution of 1825 and in the twentieth century it became a major industrial centre with the construction of the Irkutskaya dam and hydro-electric station. The early timber buildings were complemented by stone buildings from the early eighteenth century onwards but the centre was almost completely destroyed by fire in 1879. The Trans-Siberian Railway arrived in 1898.

On our arrival at Irkutsk, as ever exactly on time, we were all desperate for a shower and hair wash, having spent two days without either and sort of washing with wet wipes. However, a proper wash would have to wait until we arrived in the village of Listvyanka.

Howard was leaving us at Irkutsk to go on a horse riding trek and so changed into his riding boots and hard hat - where had he hidden those in his luggage? - and walked down the station platform all ready for the off! However, he was a day out and was to stay with us until the following day.

We looked down the platform of the large and busy station, brightly painted in green and cream, for someone holding a JGR sign with our names and eventually caught sight of Ivan from the Baikal Mystery Travel Company who would be our guide for this part of our adventure. Ivan had learned his superb English in Russia but with an American accent, had travelled in the UK and was good at his job. He told us he used to guide on the Trans-Siberian journey so had completed that over forty times. Whilst for Russians using aircraft for the journey was cheaper he explained that Russians are very nervous flyers and prefer to stay on the ground.

Ivan drove along a good quality road leading nowhere other than Lake Baikal and the settlements on the shore of the lake. We were to stay for one night only in the one road in and no road out lakeside village settlement of Listvyanka, approximately thirty miles from Irkutsk. As we went Ivan told us that Baikal is the world's largest freshwater lake and has three hundred rivers flowing into it but only one, the Angara, flowing outwards. We stopped to see the mysterious Shaman Rock at the start of the Angara but it was covered in mist and not visible and we never did sight it.

Ivan took us into Listvyanka and up a road in a side valley, valleys such as these being where most of the buildings were situated. He drove past an ugly four storey concrete building, one of the very few concrete buildings in the village, and stopped outside a Swiss chalet style building with balconies. We were greeted by the host Tatania with much welcomed and needed coffee and biscuits and relaxed in the comfortable and clean log-lined interior.

Ivan left us and we immediately showered and freshened up and then, with Howard now changed out of his riding gear, went to explore the village. Dwellings, most with a full log store outside, lined a series of valleys running away from the lake with tree covered hills behind and with the lake shoreline having restaurants, food stalls and entertainments and a picnic area at the far end as well as a school with a brightly coloured fence of pencil shaped staves. Overall, the village had the atmosphere of a typical seaside resort such as Margate or Southend. We wandered around, saw the keels of the moored boats and the lake bottom through the crystal clear waters and watched two semi-clad young women dancing in unison on a first floor balcony for some sort of filming session, with an accompanying live band on the shore line. Even in summer they must have been cold! Finding a café we ordered omul, a fish unique to Lake Baikal, and vegetables and then disputed the bill which had acquired errors due to us changing our order mid-way. Eventually all was resolved. Walking back along the front I bought some souvenir matryoshka dolls and we then returned to the chalet for a rest. There we found our train tickets for the next stage of the train journey waiting for us, helpfully left by Ivan.

Leaving Howard to have a doze June and I went back outside for another walk. We chatted in sign language with a family on the beach, sharing photos of our respective children. We gazed again through the absolutely clear lake water to the sandy bottom and we tried to locate the church which was listed as a tourist sight but we failed to find the right road. Then as we wandered along the promenade we suddenly heard a roar and a screech as a Lada Riva car with four hefty men on board raced up a stream bed from the beach, under a bridge supporting the shore road, up a bank, over the shore road and back down onto the beach, round and round and round. Then the vehicle got stuck on a rock hidden in the beach mud and all the occupants got out to push. June and I decided that alcohol must be involved somewhere! A young German couple standing with us watching this escapade and travelling on the Trans-Siberian from east to west, the opposite way to us, and from Beijing to Moscow, agreed with our assessment. As we stood there we were approached by a down and out man for money, which we declined to give. It was noticeable throughout Russia that there were many beggars, often including old ladies. Walking on we noted the well-kept memorials to the fallen of both world wars.

Listvyanka was the first time on the trip that we encountered rain, not hard rain but a light drizzle, and we could tell that the lake, surrounded as it was by mountains, had its own microclimate. Also, being surrounded by mountains, the only good mobile signal was on the shoreline. As dusk came a mist hung over the lake, making it look ever so beautiful and mysterious.

Returning to the accommodation we found an additional guest staying, a Japanese lady tour organiser. Apparently Japanese visitors are common in this area since, after the Second World War, the Great Patriotic War, many, many Japanese prisoners of war were kept captive by the Soviets and died in Siberia. Having a bit of time to relax I was able to re-sort and tidy all my luggage, much needed after living out of a bag for the last several days. Each of us seemed to have a different approach to luggage and clothing. June had brought a suitcase and a backpack with enough clothes for the whole trip. Howard travelled lighter and washed his clothes in each hotel, sometimes having to carry items outside his rucksack to finish drying and to air in the open. I decided that I wasn't carrying a bag full of dirty washing all the way to Vladivostok and threw away each day's underwear and other clothes when they reached the end of their usefulness, all from Primark so inexpensive. This, and the consumption of the food I had brought with me, gave me space in my bags to carry small souvenirs home.

The next morning, Sunday, after a good night's sleep and another shower, I appeared for breakfast and found that we were joined at the table by Natalie, a Buryat who grew up in Listvyanka but now lived in Japan and had returned to the place of her upbringing for a holiday. Buryats are the local and numerous indigenous people of the area and have a Shamanistic and Buddhist culture, much ravaged by the years of communism. After breakfast I opened the Father's Day cards that I had tucked away in my bags and took a photograph of them from my bedroom balcony, with the village in the background, to show later, at home, where I was on the day.

With a bit of time to spare after breakfast Howard and I walked further up the chalet road while June had time to herself. As we walked into the woods we found an older man digging up wild flowers which, in a sign language chat with him, he told us he would take home for his dining table. Remembering the warnings in the Lonely Planet and Bryn Thomas books about ticks, which can carry encephalitis, we kept our sleeves long and covered as much bare skin as possible. As we wandered back there were a couple of cows loose in the road together with a few stray dogs. This was in contrast to the most noticeable general absence of farm animals, birds and even flies and spiders on the journey so far.

Once back we compared our itineraries to see when June and I would again see Howard and we exchanged e-mail addresses so we could keep in touch with each other once home. Then, with Howard dressed in riding boots and hat again and with our goodbyes, he was collected for his horse riding trek. He would be following on to Vladivostok a day behind us. It was sad to separate from Howard and we missed him on the last leg of the journey but fortunately June was a brilliant companion as well. All three of our characters complemented each other and I learned much from both. Three can give a difficult social dynamic but we clicked together. Howard was very relaxed and even when we almost missed our train in Ekaterinberg his only comment was

'Well, JGR will need to sort it out and make sure we have somewhere to stay.' He seemed unfazed by problems or difficulties and was prepared to push boundaries. June was more like me and wanted to know the 'whys and wherefores' but was braver in most respects and more sociable when meeting other travellers on the way. Both were more discerning in who could and couldn't be befriended and trusted. In their different ways they both educated and trained me in the fine art of exploration and I am grateful to them for that.

A little while after Howard's departure Ivan called for June and me and we loaded our luggage into his car and jumped in. Another tourist, Vanessa from Alaska, was with him, having a holiday from her job as a special needs teacher to Inuit children.

Together Ivan drove us to the Talsy Museum of Wooden Architecture, half way back to Irkutsk. The museum was uncrowded and was interesting, even if old fashioned to our minds. It consisted of a collection of traditional local Russian buildings, relocated to avoid destruction from the rising river waters at the Angara hydro-electric dam, as well as Buryat yurts and a few buildings from elsewhere in Siberia. As we went around the museum the temperature was 38C and we were glad of our hats. We stopped after an hour or so at the on-site café where we bought a good lunch of meat dumplings and sour cream followed by pancakes with ice cream and toffee sauce. At the end of the museum tour Vanessa collected her things from Ivan's car and we waited until another vehicle turned up and took her on board to continue her own schedule elsewhere.

We headed back onto the highway into central Irkutsk and drove around the city seeing some typical Soviet blocks of flats as well as older timber pre-revolution buildings. Ivan said that these timber buildings were due to be demolished in the 1970s but were saved for heritage reasons. However, they were not connected to utilities. Also, Russians preferred to live in the ugly concrete flats and away from the mouse and rat infestations which are common in the pretty timber dwellings. Mysterious fires would often destroy one of the old buildings, leaving just charred timbers around brick chimney stacks where the roof had once been, and leading to inevitable redevelopment.

After parking up Ivan took us to Irkutsk's central square where government offices were located with hammer and sickles, modernist sculptures of workers and five pointed stars adorning the freeze above the mock-Classical entrance. These offices stood in the place of a previous Orthodox cathedral which had been blown up by the communists, which was in line with a bit of a theme of theirs. After walking us along the river bank and past the post-communist reinstated statue of Alexander III, a statue of Lenin and the war memorial with its eternal flame, we had a tour of the local history museum.

Towards the end of the afternoon Ivan delivered us to a 1960s brick walled five storey block of flats with its bare concrete staircase, heavy metal external door and similar doors to each of the dwellings. Generally, Irkutsk seemed to have fewer of the typical Soviet high rise blocks of flats. This flat was to be our homestay for the night except that we weren't staying with a family and the owner didn't live there. Another British couple were there, departing that evening, as well as the flat owner, Olga, who actually lived elsewhere in the city in her mother-in-law's home. Ivan went his way and over a coffee we got chatting with Olga and she revealed that she cared for her husband's mother and had two adult daughters and worried for them, especially the daughter with a layabout husband. Family concerns can be similar the world over, for our children and for elderly parents. This homestay was used to the maximum capacity and I found myself given a bed in the enclosed balcony, which was fine in summer.

Olga left us and, being very near to the city centre, June and I went exploring. There was an interesting photographic exhibition showing old Czarist Irkutsk in the city square which we spent a fair time browsing. Following on from that we walked again along the river front, watching people fish off the small beach. We started looking for somewhere to have an evening meal, passing the usual groups of youths out on the town, but reached a consensus that we both needed to limit what we spent and so found a supermarket, bought food for the evening and for the coming train journey, and then walked back to the flat to enjoy a simple shared dinner of cooked meats, salad and yoghurts.

The next day, Monday, we were up early, before six o'clock in the morning. Olga was already there and we had a decent breakfast of bread, tomatoes, cucumbers and bellinis with sour cream and jam and slices of orange as well as coffee. We packed our bags and the trusty Ivan collected us and took us to the train station for the 7.55am train. With Olga's good breakfast inside us we felt we were ready for this final section of the journey. This was to be the longest, lasting three days and three nights.

THE HOME RUN

AT IRKUTSK TRAIN STATION June and I were directed by Ivan to the right platform and train and then, saying goodbye and thank you to him, we fished out our passports and with paper tickets in hand - again, thank you Ivan - we found the right carriage and were checked on board and shown to our compartment. This was situated at the end of the carriage and next to the provodnitsas' accommodation. We would get to know our provodnitsas as Irina and Svetlana. Their uniforms were similar to those of the provodnitsas in the first train from Moscow to Ekaterinberg but the standard of the train was similar to that from Ekaterinberg to Irkutsk. This time, since it was only June and me, we were in a two-berth compartment with June taking the bottom bunk. Again, the train was not an express but rumbled along steadily through the many, many miles towards Vladivostok.

The first part of the journey, in the broad morning daylight, was spent glued to the carriage window as we went around the beautiful coastline of Lake Baikal, crossing over the many rivers by means of steel girdered bridges, and then heading into hilly country with snow-capped mountains in the distance. It was here that we first noticed guard huts and soldiers protecting each bridge and tunnel due, we thought, to the proximity of the border with China. We passed many datcha villages here, as we did outside towns and cities throughout the journey. As the journey settled into routine and we sorted ourselves out the provodnitsa Irina came and tried to teach us some Russian, although I focused principally on refreshing my knowledge of the Cyrillic alphabet and pronouncing the letters of this.

Eventually the train pulled into the very unattractive - as far as could be seen from the train - town of Ulan Ude and we were able to disembark for a while onto the platform of the blue and beige painted station. Along with other passengers and Irina we jumped off the platform and across the tracks to get to the food stalls on the opposite platform, having looked carefully to make sure no other trains were moving around. Returning we watched with some fascination as a workman went beneath the train with a hammer, checking for metal fatigue by tapping each wheel.

Irina offered to take a photograph of June and me, at which point both June and I realised that a 'situation' was in danger of arising. How could we explain to Irina that we were travelling companions and not romantically attached to each other? With some gesticulation to my wedding ring and a shaking of the head and a pulling out of my family photograph from my wallet we managed to get the truth across. Irina then asked, by crossing her arms with her hands on her shoulders and by bowing her head, if my wife was dead. 'Nyet' was an easy answer that I could manage!

After pulling out of Ulan Ude June and I stood in the carriage corridor and made conversation of sorts with some of the other passengers. Pavel had some English and told us that after four years in the army he became a marketing manager for Red Bull serving the area from Irkutsk eastward to Chita. Fishing was his hobby. He shared photos of his family with us. Sergei worked out of Khabarovsk driving the huge diggers in the open cast mines. Proudly he showed us pictures of his five month old son and we learned that Russian men are very proud of their children. Also his sister was leaving London that very day to go back to the USA as a student. Then there was a middle aged man who wouldn't speak or engage with us at all but spent the time just looking out of the corridor window. We labelled him as a spy. As we chatted to Irina the provodnitsa we got to know her a little more and learned that she was a widow and her home town was the city of Novosibirsk which, as she assured us many times, we know not why, had a very, very good skating rink. At one station stop she took us to photograph an elderly man on the platform with some sort of very illustrious medal on his jacket but we could not make out from Irina's description what this could be.

Over the next few hours, as the train motored on, our

compartment became a social whirl. From somewhere June produced a book of coarse jokes, from exactly where I don't know. She showed it around and both Pavel and Irina immediately said Russians don't read such things and handed it back.

I felt a little like a zoo attraction and fairly soon tired of all the company, more so than did June who seemed to thrive on it. I made my excuses and wandered up the train to the restaurant car to read and daydream in peace and quiet. I asked the restaurant assistant manning the car for a 7UP but she brought me a coke, indicating that they had no 7UP. I didn't want the coke so she came back with a fizzy orange. I didn't want the fizzy orange. At that point I stood, smiled, picked up the fizzy orange and indicated that she should follow me as I went up the restaurant car to the fridge, which I then left her to open. There I was able to view their full range of drinks and finally chose a bitter lemon and paid and then sat quietly reading at one of the tables and away from the hustle and bustle of the compartment.

As well as the restaurant car there was a regular trolley service perambulating up and down the corridors every couple of hours and selling chocolate bars, the essential pot noodle type snacks and drinks. For no apparent reason June and I nicknamed the lady host of this trolley Florence. However, generally we used up our own supplies, augmented by platform vendor purchases, and keeping a routine of breakfast, lunch and evening meal, all a mixture of tins of fruit, pot noodles, soup and biscuits.

As evening came I tried to send some text messages home but on this section of the journey my mobile 'phone had very poor and sporadic signal and my attempts at communication failed. The air cooled with nightfall and as it did so it began to rain, obscuring the view outside, and so we settled down for the night. My ablutions made Irina laugh. As I washed my smelly feet with wet wipes she took me to the wc and lifted her own foot into the wash basin to show me what to do. I somehow explained that I thought I was too old to lift my leg like that and it would hurt my back. However, she was very persuasive and I ended up washing my feet in the basin as told. Irina then brought both June and me a pair of paper slippers each. With my feet now clean I pushed June out into the corridor while I changed into my night things and then stood in the corridor while June changed into hers. Our last task before getting into our bunks to sleep was to toast Howard as an absent friend and also, importantly, to celebrate another time zone.

We awoke the next day, Tuesday, and settled into our daily routine, but broken by a child, two or three years old, who would look round our compartment door to sneak a peek at us and then rush away.

Pavel and Sergei left the train at some point and the social scene thankfully diminished. Huge amounts of time were spent looking out of the window at the amazing distant scenery, more arid than previously, and gazing at the unnamed river that ran alongside the railway line for several hundred miles and then observing the occasional prison compound. Also, there were some large electric stations, placed in the middle of nowhere, but which I assumed were to power the railway. Elsewhere there were random sidings or lone workmen in hi-vis jackets walking alongside the track and again miles and miles from any civilization. We passed without stopping through numerous villages with their timber houses becoming less ornate with each mile eastwards, as did the dachas.

The day went slowly with the occasional stop allowing us to disembark but overnight the train driver speeded up, trying to make up the hour that we had slipped behind schedule, and so our night's sleep was disturbed by being thrown around all over the place with the increased rocking of the carriage. Again, as I lay in my upper berth, trying not to be shaken out onto the floor, I was aware of many goods trains passing us, this time carrying timber logs.

Wednesday came, starting with an overcast sky and a change of scenery from fairly flat to hilly, with the trees changing to include oaks as well as birch and pine. We stopped for varying lengths of time at many drab towns and villages, including the station at Yerofei Pavlovich, painted brown and grey with dogs' head statues. Originally, I assumed that there was a link to the Pavlov of Pavlov's dogs fame but actually the town is named after Yerofei Pavlovich Khabarov, the ruthless seventeenth century explorer. We stopped for a while at the city station of Birobidzhan with signage in both Russian and Hebrew. This settlement was a left over from Stalin's attempt to create a Jewish homeland in the USSR but now with very few Jews remaining after waves of emigration out of the country, including to Israel. However, there was insufficient time there to leave the station area and explore. Sometimes the stops were only for a couple of minutes, just long enough to set down passengers and gather up those waiting on the platform. At other times the stops were thirty or forty-five minutes, giving plenty of time to browse the platform stalls for something to eat.

Towards the end of the afternoon we looked in awe as we crossed the great Amur River, with its huge mile long bridge over the water and the now usual guard boxes, and then we pulled into the major city of Khabarovsk, again named after Yerofei Pavlovich, for a longer, hour's length stop.

Pulling away from Khabarovsk my Russian lessons with Irina continued, moving on from counting from zero to ten to learning the days of the week. She gave a boxed bottle of expensive looking scent to June that made June very wary. Not only did June not want it or need it but she felt if she so much as opened the box Irina would expect full payment to be made. It was left well alone on the compartment table.

As we moved further east and then south towards our final destination the climate changed and it became consistently cooler with more regular and constant rainfall. Everything was that little bit greener. Mountains were present in the distance which we realised must be in China and my mobile 'phone switched from a Russian to a Chinese network. We tried to look at the changed scenery but it was becoming dusk and soon night fell.

The train must have been delayed yet again because it was speeding along and swaying badly from side to side. When I went to settle down into my upper berth on this last night on board the train even Irina must have been concerned that I would be thrown down to the floor. She produced some leather straps to keep me safe, not by tying me in but to go from the open side of the berth up to the ceiling to close the gap. I wondered how I would negotiate those if I needed a night visit to the toilet but fortunately did not have the need. Despite the train movement I slept well.

At five o'clock the next morning, Thursday, I fumbled around to turn off the alarm I had set on my mobile 'phone. It was still dark but it was time to put on my valuables belt bag from next to me, get up and be dressed and packed ready for our arrival at the end of the line, at Vladivostok. June and I cleared our respective berths, gathered our bedding together and, as before, followed everyone else in the carriage to a big, big pile of dirty linen at the end of the corridor outside the provodnitsas' compartment and dumped ours on top, ready to be taken away for laundering.

Carefully checking that nothing was left behind we got ready to leave. As we said goodbye to Irina she asked for my ticket once more and wrote on the back something in Russian. Only recently has a friendly Russian speaker I know kindly translated this for me as saying 'With best wishes, happiness, health, love, success. Provodnitsa Irina' although interpretation of the hand-written Russian was difficult even for my translator. Again, the train arrived at Vladivostok absolutely on time at 6.17am and we disembarked and looked around. Finding what we wanted at the end of the platform we wandered along and took the obligatory photograph of the finishing post, a monument topped with the Russian double headed eagle, telling us that we were 9,288 kilometers from Moscow. Even as we took the photograph the train was leaving the station for the sidings ready for cleaning, restocking and then, in only a few hours, heading back westwards.

We made our way from the deep platform cutting up the station stairs to ground level and had our first sight of the city, originally founded in 1860 as a Russian military outpost with its name meaning 'Lord of the East'. As we were to find out over the next day Vladivostok is a port city, originally with a very multicultural population and the home of first the Russian, then the Soviet and now again the Russian Pacific Fleet as well as fishing fleets since it is largely, although not completely, ice free in winter. Construction of the Trans-Siberian Railway began in Vladivostok in 1891 and was completed in 1904. After the October 1917 revolution the Japanese occupied the city until 1922. From 1930 to 1992 it was a closed city and foreigners were not allowed to enter.

As June and I left the station a man with a sign collected us and drove us to the multi-storey Azimut Hotel, a distance of under one kilometer and which we could easily have walked. However, I supposed that JGR wanted to make sure we arrived there safely and didn't head off in the completely wrong direction, to spend our stay lost around the back streets of the city.

We booked into the hotel, again having our passports photocopied, found our rooms - mine was on the fifth floor, June's on the floor below - had the so, so good shower and freshen up, met again for breakfast in the hotel restaurant and then were collected from the hotel reception at 8am - yes, 8am - by Alexander, our local guide and a lifelong resident of the city. He drove us to the university, the Eagles Nest Hill with its view over the harbour and the part-completed Golden Horn bridge, this being constructed for the 2012 APEC economic meeting of heads of state. We were taken to the top of the funicular railway, which we didn't go on, but standing there gave us a good view of a loaded lorry burning its clutch out trying to get up the steep road next to it. Then we dropped down the hill to the large main city square and explored the S56 Second World War submarine sitting on the dockside, the adjacent large war memorial with its obligatory eternal flame and the more recently rebuilt monument commemorating the visit of the last Czar, the original having been removed by the communists. There are other attractions in

Vladivostok, some a little way out of the city centre such as the Fortress, the Primorsky Picture Gallery, the Arsevev Regional Museum and the Voroshilov Battery on Russky Island but these were not included in our itinerary and we did not see these.

Alexander returned us to the hotel through the noticeably busy Vladivostok traffic and as we went in we were confronted by lots of very loud Chinese tourists. June and I took time out and away from each other to relax and I went to the hotel's 'business centre', a small cubicle off the reception area with glazed partitioning around and most importantly a computer, so that I could send an e-mail home, the first of the trip. The hotel reception wanted to charge me for a whole hour's use but since I had only been ten minutes we went through a difficult negotiation before they agreed to settle for a suitably proportionate sum.

June and I met up again and we wandered around the city centre, had a coffee in the GUM store overlooking the main square, browsed the bric-a-brac stores on the front where a shopkeeper tried to sell June some medals, the offer of which June declined, explaining to me that they might not be genuine and if they were they may not be allowed out of the country. Being arrested at the airport was something she wished to avoid! We then headed for a local open market but that was the moment when I started feeling unwell and so, making sure June was content, I headed back to the hotel, only ten minutes away, and rested. I soon recovered and a little while later we went out to look at the town again, found a café and ate and then continued our explorations. We realised how limited the city centre was and in fact the whole city, which is a typical port and, in my opinion, not worth a visit on its own merits. Back at the hotel we arranged to meet later in the bar.

The bar was busy and dressed up youngsters arrived for some sort of function in a back room. Also in the building but with a separate external entrance was some form of strip joint but we did not see whether that was busy or not. As we sat in the bar June noticed another couple of Brits - how did she know? - and got chatting with them and they invited us to join them. Martin and Michael were both in their late fifties and were trying to motorbike around the world in six months in support of the Worcester and Northamptonshire Air Ambulance and The Myton Hospices. They had arrived in Vladivostok three weeks before and were waiting, with diminishing patience, for their motorbikes to clear the Vladivostok docks to where they had been shipped from America. They had quickly exhausted all there was to do in the city and were now bored and frustrated and keen to get off for a ride through Mongolia. As we talked they educated June and me in the dynamics of the hotel reception. They entertained themselves by playing a game of 'spotting the Chinese secret service agents' who minded and kept watch on the Chinese tourists and apparently stayed awake in reception all night to make sure none of their countrymen escaped and defected! Later in the evening we were joined by Jean, a Frenchman known to Martin and Michael, who was biking around the world as well. It was a very pleasant final evening in Russia.

However, eventually the evening had to end and before settling down to sleep in my room I decided to have a final coffee of the day but realised that I only had sparkling water with which to make it. So I did and it was a very strange drink I had but it didn't make me ill and didn't disturb my sleep!

I woke up on the last day, Friday, suitably rested. I showered and headed down to reception, met June and we tried to work out when we thought Howard would arrive. Based on the time of our arrival we thought he may already be in the hotel but when we checked at the reception desk he had not yet booked in. We headed to breakfast, were allowed into the hotel dining room by the staff once we had shown our room keys and as we ate we checked our itinerary. This was short and simple. A taxi would turn up at 11am to take us the thirty miles to the airport for our 2.15pm flight to Moscow. Breakfast finished we decided we had time to head down to the nearby beach on the Amursky Bay side of town, away from the harbour. We strolled along the sand and had a paddle in the Sea of Japan. One thought on our minds was to find the aquarium but when we asked directions from a local, who amusingly called it the fish museum, we decided it was too far away for the short time we had. We strolled back to the hotel and packed. I carefully checked that nothing was left behind and then booked out at reception and waited with June, first for Howard if he appeared, so we could say 'hello' and 'goodbye', and then for our taxi.

June and I thought we would miss Howard but just as we had given up hope he arrived and it was good to see him again. Our time together was short since he needed to find his room and wash off the effects of the three day train journey before he was collected by Alexander and taken for his own tour of Vladivostok.

With Howard gone to sort himself out June and I settled down to reflect on our Tran-Siberian experience as we waited for our taxi. We waited. And waited. 11.15 came and no taxi. 11.30 came and no taxi. We began to worry. Would this be another 'Ekaterinberg?' Missing a flight would be far worse than missing a train. Our visas would expire, we would have 'Overstay' stamped on our passports and we would run out of money. Anxiety began to build in both of us and there were only two of us to share the worry, with no Howard to calm us down. We glanced at each other and then suddenly I put all my fears and anxiety to one side. I resolved to be decisive and act. We would make our own way to the airport. I got out of the chair and marched over to the reception desk and asked them to order us a taxi and they immediately made a telephone call. I had hardly returned to my chair when the reception staff called over to tell us that our just booked taxi had arrived. It must have been waiting at the head of the service road. We thanked reception and speedily walked out, gave our destination to the driver, put our bags in the boot and with June in the back and me in the front and the time being 11.40 we set off.

Our driver didn't speak English but was amiable. Trying to get out of Vladivostok we got stuck in traffic and glanced anxiously at our watches, mentally urging the driver to put his foot down. Nevertheless, we were sure things would speed up once we were on the motorway. They did speed up but not as much as we wanted. The motorway was undergoing major works and we had to race along a parallel three lane temporary aggregate trackway with no lane markings but with vast clouds of dust. It was hairy but we survived and to be honest didn't care as long as we got to the airport in time.

As we swung into the airport car park June and I started working out how we were going to pay the driver, both of us being short of cash. The taxi came to a halt and the fare was 1,500 roubles. June didn't have enough cash but I had just sufficient so took responsibility for paying while June retrieved our bags from the rear. I remembered to get a receipt and then yelling 'spasiba' to the taxi man we ran to the modern glass-clad airport building. It was just gone 1pm. Before entering inside all visitors had to pass through one of two metal detectors gates. There was no queue. Instead, we were confronted with a mob, a situation much worse than that at Ekaterinberg. There the crowd had been in lines. Here it was a disorderly rabble. We got ourselves prepared with plastic trays already grabbed for electrical and metal items and then forced our way to the metal detector gates while our bags and trays went through a scanner. 1.15pm.

On the other side we found the Aeroflot desk, showed our passports and booking information and got our boarding cards and June deposited her hold luggage. 1.25pm.

Then we followed the signs and headed up the escalator and presented passports at border control. With passports checked we headed for departures only to be confronted with another hindrance. There was a further security check. So, electrics and metal items into trays again and then everything through the scanner and us through metal detector gates. My bag was pulled to one side by a determined female security guard who wanted it unlocked which I did for her. She then started rummaging through the contents and disturbing all my careful packing and getting cross in the process. I tried to help by motioning 'let me' but there was no engagement. June said to me 'Just let her get on with it. Now is not the moment for trouble'. I obeyed June and let the guard continue until she found my travel kettle element and pulled it out, examined it, was satisfied and put it back, leaving me to repack my bag. 1.40pm.

Through the other side of security we checked the departure boards and went to the relevant gate. 1.45pm and just in time by a couple of minutes to board the second and last bus to take us across the tarmac to the aeroplane. We had had no time to spare but had made it. I pushed to the back of my mind what would have happened if we had delayed ordering the taxi by only a few minutes more and regretted that I waited as long as I did before doing so. Once back in the UK I wrote to JGR asking for the taxi fare back which they returned without any problem. They explained that the taxi company they used had made a mistake, putting the flight departure time of 2.15pm down as the hotel pick up time!

The flight departed on time with my heart still thumping and racing with the stress and with the subsequent relief at catching it. June and I had not been allocated seats together but once the seat belt signs were off we met in the aisle at regular intervals.

It was a long, long flight back to Moscow, half way around the world from Vladivostok and it would last for nine hours. I had a window seat and spent a great number of those nine hours looking down at the lakes, rivers and forests below. A young Russian lady was next to me and a few times I tried to engage her in conversation but with no response. Each to their own. A palatable in-flight meal was served, I had a couple of coffees from the trolley and roughly on time we landed back at Moscow Sheremetyevo, last seen by us twelve days before and where we had a four hour stop over. That was plenty of time to exit the internal flights side of the airport, obtain boarding cards from the Aeroflot desk and go through security again, this time without any issues, through border control where our passports were stamped and landing cards handed in and then it was time to orientate ourselves, find a coffee and a sandwich and sit in front of the departures screen patiently waiting. As an aside, we later found out that Howard had lost his landing card which gave him real problems with emigration but they did let him out in the end!

The flight back to London was straightforward, this time with both June and me sitting together in the shaking, rattling back row of the plane next to the toilets behind us. We were too tired to worry or care. Our fellow passenger in the row of three was an English lady who did engage with us in conversation. Her husband was based in Moscow and she alternated two weeks in London followed by two weeks in Moscow's expat quarter. Whilst she had got to know a couple of French women generally she felt lonely in Russia. She found Moscow hard work and wanted to gain a circle of friends there but her attempts to start a WI branch had met with only a poor response.

I clutched the arms of the aeroplane seat as we landed at Heathrow on time at just before 10pm. Being at the back of the plane it took ages to disembark into the terminal but that gave me time to turn on my mobile 'phone, have it locate my UK BT network and for me to send a text message home that I was, at last, back in the United Kingdom. Once through border control - just a flash of our passports - I waited with June until she had reclaimed her luggage.

It was time to say an emotional farewell to each other and then she headed off to catch a bus to Swindon and I headed to the underground station for the Piccadilly Line into central London, feeling suddenly very deflated. Then I realised why. I had actually been awake for over twenty-four hours, mostly travelling, without any proper sleep but of course, with the time zone changes, I hadn't realised. I wasn't so much deflated as dead tired. I changed underground trains at Hammersmith and took the District Line to Victoria main line station. I had intended to get back through Charing Cross to my home train station but decided that the time was too tight and I may miss the last train and I wanted to avoid that theme developing again! Instead, I went to Bromley South and allowed one of the waiting black London taxis to drop me at my front door. My wife opened that door to one very tired but successful and now confident traveller who had crossed 9,288 life changing kilometers, through eight out of Russia's eleven time zones, taken over 1200 photographs - as with all digital photographs a third of them were quickly deleted - and gained two friends, a deep love for Russia and her people and a thirst for more adventures! My life would never be, and has never been, the same again.

THE NEXT ADVENTURE

TRAVEL BY BOAT

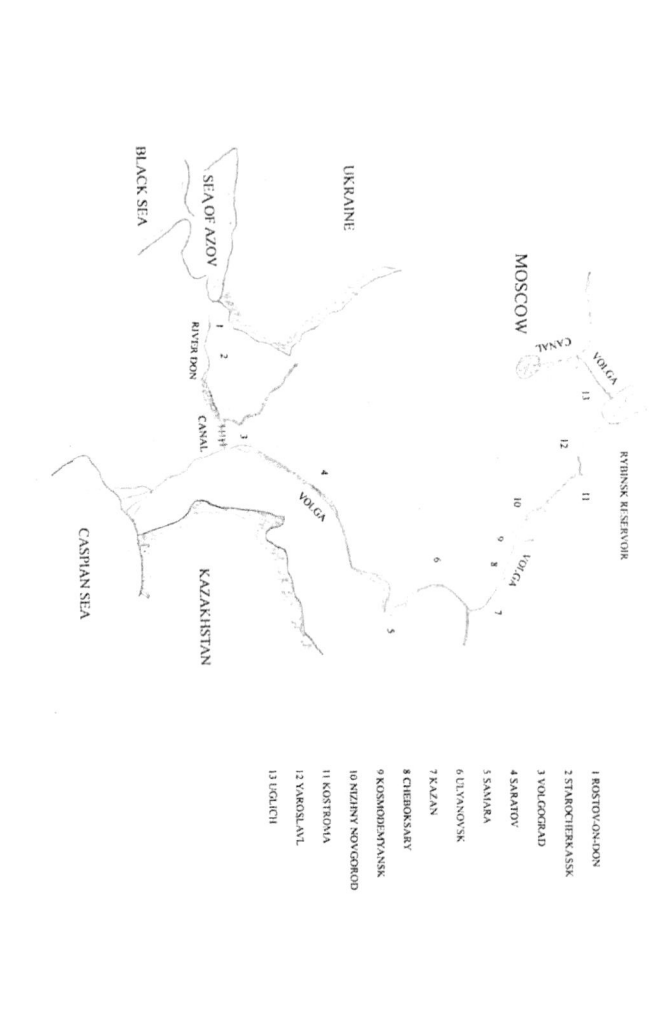

RYBINSK RESERVOIR
MOSCOW
CANAL
VOLGA
RIVER DON
CANAL
VOLGA
UKRAINE
SEA OF AZOV
BLACK SEA
CASPIAN SEA
KAZAKHSTAN

1 ROSTOV-ON-DON
2 STAROCHERKASSK
3 VOLGOGRAD
4 SARATOV
5 SAMARA
6 ULYANOVSK
7 KAZAN
8 CHEBOKSARY
9 KOSMODEMYANSSK
10 NIZHNY NOVGOROD
11 KOSTROMA
12 YAROSLAVL
13 UGLICH

DECISION OR INDECISION?

THE COLD DARK NIGHTS of winter can be difficult and many struggle when the sunshine disappears. It's been given a name - Seasonal Affective Disorder. One gets up in the dark, enjoys a few hours of daylight, sometimes full daylight but more often than not a gloomy half-light brought on by clouds and rain, and then before the end of the afternoon it's dark again. It is the time when most will want something to look forward to, something to keep them going until Spring, and it is no wonder that holiday companies launch their advertising campaigns in the depths of the winter season.

In the winter after my Trans-Siberian trip I was unsettled. I had an itch and as the saying goes 'if one has an itch then it has to be scratched'. I had lived in the 'glow' of my railway adventure for many months, boring everyone with my photographs and reminiscences, but now found that glow fading and I could not settle. That train journey was a beginning that had given me a big itch and as the months passed I became restless. I couldn't concentrate on anything. I'd start something and not finish it. I would sit down and then stand up and pace around and then sit down again. Something was missing. I needed another adventure and eventually I decided the only way to scratch the itch was to give in. My mind and energies turned to planning what I really wanted, which was a return to Russia, probably not such a big journey as the first time but nevertheless a further exploration of that enchanting country.

However, whilst I had faced down my fears and anxieties once for the train trip, would I be able to face them down a second time? To try to repeat something enjoyable can often lead to disappointment and the same insecurities as before swept over me, although this time there was a difference. This time I had experience. This time I was older and wiser, knew myself better, knew more of my strengths and my weaknesses and knew better how to go about things.

So as the dark winter nights set in at the end of 2011 I looked wistfully at the JGR website. JGR were a known quantity for me. I knew how they operated, their good points and their bad points and the precautions I would need to take, especially against missing any trains or planes! JGR offered several trips, as do many other companies of course, in winter or summer, from short city breaks to Moscow and St Petersburg, to river cruises, to various railway trips, including to Bejing through Mongolia, as well as other options.

I started thinking. I knew I didn't want to go in winter since winter in Russia is cold and dark. A slightly shorter trip than before would be preferable. A trip with JGR was likely, but not definitely, to be with other people for company. JGR were reasonably priced. JGR could sort out a visa and travel insurance. Working to those parameters gave me several options within my available budget including city breaks but, having read again the Lonely Planet and Bryn Thomas books, and browsed yet again the JGR website information, I became intrigued by the Golden Ring.

The Golden Ring is a modern title given to a number of very ancient towns within reach of, and to the north-east of, Moscow, each filled with golden onion domed churches, hence the name. The list of towns and cities is not definitive but includes Vladimir, Suzdal, Kostroma, Yaroslavl, Uglich, Rostov-Veliky, Pereslavl-Zalessky, Sergiev Posad, Ivanovo and the palace and monastery of Bogolyubovo.

The Golden Ring tour JGR offered started with a couple of days in Moscow, revisiting sights I'd already seen but would have no problem seeing again, then being driven to Vladimir and Bogolyubovo before enjoying a night in a homestay in Suzdal and then returning to Moscow. I started reading more online and in my books.

Vladimir was founded in 1108 by the Kievan Rus Prince Vladimir Monomalch and became the capital of his principality. However, in 1157, under his grandson, Andrei Bogolyubsky, the capital transferred to Suzdal. Vladimir has the ancient Assumption Cathedral, construction of which began in 1158, the smaller Cathedral of St Dmitry, built in the late tenth century, these being among the oldest church buildings in Russia, and the Golden Gate, built by Andrie Bogolyubsky, a city gate modelled on that in Kiev which was, in turn, modelled on one in Constantinople. The city of Vladimir was devastated by the Mongols after which it declined, became dependent on Moscow and never regained its previous status. Nowadays it's an industrial centre.

The Palace of Bogolyubovo was built as a fortified structure between 1158 and 1165 by the Prince Andrei Bogolyubsky mentioned above and also has a much later monastery and churches.

Suzdal is the 'jewel in the crown', the glistening must-see place in the Golden Ring. The town was a royal capital city when Moscow was still a small, insignificant riverside settlement. The first written reference to Suzdal dates from 1024. The town prospered, became the capital of its principality but was destroyed by the Mongols in the late thirteenth century. However, it was re-established and under Ivan the Terrible became a major monastic centre, all such monasteries being fortified. At one time there was a church for every twelve of its citizens as well as fifteen monasteries and even now it remains crammed with churches and monasteries. It became a major commercial centre and its early nineteenth century trading arcade survives. In the later nineteenth century it was bypassed by the Trans-Siberian Railway and thereafter fell into decline.

I was excited at the thought of seeing these sights but disappointed that I would not get to see Kazan. Kazan had become a 'holy grail' after my brief glimpse when passing through on the railway. Then I thought 'Why not?' So I asked JGR if I could do an extension to their tour to include Kazan and they quoted a side trip for me at the end of the programmed tour, suggesting the taking of a night train from Moscow, then allowing me to explore

Kazan on my own without a guide, and then returning on a sleeper train to Moscow on the evening of the same day.

I was thrilled at all of this. Now it seemed that all I had to do was pluck up the courage to have the important marital discussion. However, my wife knew what was coming, in the way that a spouse does, and gave her approval with no hesitation and I was grateful to her for that. Nevertheless, I decided to wait until after Christmas before booking.

Come January 2012 my mind had not changed. I still wanted to go and so I rechecked my budget, since with the Kazan side trip the cost had crept up, but all was satisfactory. I checked my leave status with my office, checked my family were content - did they really have a choice? - and then sat one evening in front of the home computer rereading the JGR website. All was good and I was ready to press the buttons to go - the tour, the side trip, flights, visa and travel insurance and always the sting in the tail, the single person supplement.

It was at that moment that for some unknown reason I let my eyes wander down the list of tours JGR advertised. They came to rest on a river cruise. Curiosity led me to open up the web page and read the content carefully. It told me that fourteen days could be spent cruising from Rostov-on-Don northwards up the Don and Volga rivers, finishing in Moscow and calling at all sorts of places, many of which were completely unknown to me - Rostov-on-Don itself, Starocherkassk, Volgograd, Saratov, Samara, Ulyanovsk, Kazan - yes! -, Cheboksary, Kosmodemyansk, Nizhny Novgorod, Kostroma, Yaroslavl, Uglich and finally Moscow.

Even before I pulled the atlas off the book shelf I recognised Kostroma, Yaroslavl and Uglich as Golden Ring cities. Kazan was there, so was Volgograd, formerly known as Stalingrad. I opened the atlas up, found the right page and followed the route. I flicked through the Lonely Planet and Bryn Thomas books. I had a dilemma. The cost was more than I originally intended but still affordable. I would certainly not be cruising alone but the time away from home would be longer. 'What to do?' I wondered. Then I decided. What to do was to go to bed and sleep on it. And so I did.

The next day I had a look again the options in front of me. Travelling by boat on a river seemed far better than travelling by car on a road. I would see more of Russia with the boat cruise. I would see some of the Golden Ring towns and cities and, so important for me, I would see beautiful Kazan. After sitting at my office desk all day only half concentrating on my work and mostly and privately mulling over the choices before me, the final decision was easy. River it was to be and in May.

So for a second evening that week I sat down in front of my home computer, opened up the JGR website and clicked the cruise, the single person supplement - I did offer to JGR to share if there was anyone else willing but they ignored me -, the flights, visa and insurance options, then paid a deposit by card and that was that. One cruise, on the Don and Volga rivers, fully booked!

The Volga, the longest river in Europe at 3,531 kilometers, runs from a small brook north-west of Moscow and gradually gains in size to become a strong, deep river before discharging through a delta into the Caspian Sea and now hosts some of the world's largest reservoirs, linked to hydro-electric schemes. It is connected to all of Russia's major seas by canals and carries half of the country's water freight. This was, along with other rivers such as the Don, and rivers like the Dniester and to a lesser extent the Dnieper, one of the major ancient trade routes, even bringing the Vikings southwards to the near point of the river Don and thence from that river into the Sea of Azov, the Black Sea and Byzantium. I would be going the other way, from south to north, and would not be having to carry a boat between the Don and Volga rivers as the Vikings did, since these are now joined by a ship canal opened in 1952 and built by German prisoners of war.

For a few days after booking I was on a 'high' but then the reality of everyday life brought me back down to earth. I started to prepare by reading about where I was going. I started the visa application process with JGR and again went to their offices but this time handed over my passport, completed forms and photographs with no hesitation and with confidence that I would get my passport back. A couple of weeks later I picked up my passport with the visa inserted.

Over time JGR sent out by e-mail a more detailed itinerary with other general information including flight details with British Airways and the name of the boat, the Anton Chekhov. I was able to get a deck plan of the boat online and print that off and also saw bits of it on various YouTube clips and found out that it was actually built in Austria for cruising on the Danube. Many off boat tours were shown on the itinerary and I was unclear whether these were organised by JGR or the boat. A quick telephone call to JGR told me that the boat organised all of these and I was content with that.

Everything was set and had so far been stress free but as I spent those months looking forward to a return to Russia the rest of life was falling apart. The most immediate concern was a formal employment process that my line manager, with whom I had a personality clash, started against me, I think to try to force me out of my job. Sadly such managers do still exist. Discussions and negotiations between my trade union and my employer's Head of HR took place over a couple of months. The cost of this to me was to increase my anxiety levels and aggravate my depression with on and off episodes of self-doubt and the full range of other typical symptoms. The list of these is long but included panic attacks, brain fog, insomnia, indecision, inability to concentrate, forgetfulness, weight loss, hyperventilation, gastric issues, physical shaking and crippling mental and physical fatigue. Sometimes I had only one of these, sometimes a combination, and thankfully only rarely did I seem to have all together. However, I knew I was ill. Yet all the time, alongside this, I had the welcome distraction of progressing my plans for my new adventure.

I was able to get a map off the shelf at Stanford, one of the excellent World Mapping Project series, showing the western regions of Russia through which I would be travelling, as well as ordering maps in Cyrillic for Volgograd and Kazan. I would not need any food for the journey nor any more inoculations. I reflected on my train journey experience, reread my diary from that trip and followed up some of the notes I had made. I made sure I had what I learned was useful - a torch, carrier bags, lots of AA batteries, a watch for GMT and a separate watch for local time, plenty of credit on my mobile 'phone for text messages to and from home and, most importantly, a pair of flipflops.

Also I obtained a decent sized notebook, hardback for durability, and to be used as a diary and to keep essential information including some basic Russian vocabulary, although only three words in Russian - da, nyet and spaseba, yes, no and thank you - seem adequate for getting by and these were my mainstay on the Trans-Siberian. On later trips I would also add flight details, passport and travel insurance numbers, home e-mails and 'phone numbers into the notebook for easy reference. I noted the need for water and for keeping to a sensible diet to avoid digestive issues. I looked out my ukelele - for personal use only and not for public performance! I spent an evening snipping and pasting together Google maps of each place the boat would visit except those for which I had purchased maps. I looked out my previous Moscow maps. I booked a taxi to take me to the airport.

Yet as I packed and repacked my excitement and anticipation were marred by my work situation which was reaching a climax right at the time I was to go away. On the one hand I was having meetings and negotiations and preparing paperwork to protect my employment. On the other hand I was busy checking the tour details and carefully packing so I could travel on hand luggage only. I was being pulled in several different directions. However, on the working day before I was due to depart my employer's Head of HR told me that the formal employment process against me was being suspended for ever in favour of mediation and that he never wanted to be dealing with a matter of such a nature as this again. He wished me well for my trip and told me to relax and enjoy it. As soon as I absorbed what he was saying I did as he told me and after breathing a sigh of relief I really did relax.

HEADING SOUTH

ON THE LAST DAY of April 2012, a Monday, just before 5am, as dawn was getting ready to break, my prebooked taxi arrived outside the house. As soon as I saw it pull up I opened the front door, said goodbye to my wife, who had managed to stagger out of bed to see me off, left my daughter, who had not staggered out of bed, sound asleep, showed my passport to the driver and jumped into the car with my hand luggage bag, drawstring bag and, of course, my ukulele. With a slight feeling of trepidation I was, nevertheless, on my way.

As we drove off the driver and I chatted. I sympathised with him for the early start and he told me that he preferred to work nights since the driving conditions were easier with fewer vehicles on the roads. To my surprise we took a cross town route to Heathrow Airport through Streatham, Wandsworth, Kew and only then onto the motorway - the M4 - for the last stretch to Terminal Five, the terminal serving British Airways with whom all my flights had been booked by JGR. Equally surprising was the speed of the journey which took only forty-five minutes. That was just as well because my Terminal Five experience was not to be straight forward.

I thanked and paid the taxi driver and walked into the terminal building and found an automatic check-in point which firmly rejected my booking reference details. With some difficulty I managed to find a uniformed real person but my pleas for help were not heeded and instead I was sent to a different zone of the airport, for what reason I don't know. With some effort I managed to track down a second uniformed real person who this time was just what I needed. She entered my booking reference into the machine and it was again rejected but she then tried a few other things and eventually managed to enter me through my passport number. My boarding card was printed out and with thanks and a sigh of relief I headed off through the entry gates and joined a fairly lengthy queue to go through security. Having done this before I was familiar with, and prepared for, the process - electrics and liquids, not much, only a small shampoo and hand cleaner, into tray, watch and wallet into gilet, gilet and fleece off and into the tray, shoes off and into tray, belt bag, drawstring bag, hand luggage bag and ukulele into trays. A check of pockets for anything metallic I may have forgotten then trays placed onto the conveyor belt while I queued at the metal detector gate. Once on the other side of that gate various of my trays came through and I reversed the process, putting shoes, gilet and belt bag back on. My drawstring bag came through but there was no sign of my hand luggage bag to which my ukulele was tied. Then I noticed that it was in the charge of a nice uniformed lady who brought it to the counter and called me over to undo the padlock so she could search inside. Again, it was my travel kettle element she wanted to look at and I should have put that with my electrical things. I resolved that next time - next time? - I must put that where it could be easily seen.

I was grateful that I had allowed lots of time at the airport and that the taxi journey was quick. That kept my anxiety levels under control. Now I had a couple of hours to spare so I orientated myself, found the gate locations and departure boards and then got myself a Starbucks coffee and three small bottles of water and sat and read. A second coffee followed the first before the gate information was displayed.

Making sure all my belongings were with me I wandered through the busy airport and joined other passengers gathering at the relevant place. Smiling staff welcomed me on board what, I was pleased to see, was a Boing 747 and on finding my allocated middle seat I saw that there were not many other passengers, with only one other in my row of ten seats. I wondered how many other JGR customers were on this flight.

The plane doors were closed, seat belts put on and seats rearranged upright with arm rests down. We taxied to the end of the runway, paused for a moment and then I shut my eyes and gripped the seat arms as we raced into the air. Only when some way off the ground was I brave enough to open my eyes and move to the vacant window seat to admire the view below with little trees and fields and houses and with little cars and trains moving around.

We levelled off and the stewards came round offering free drinks, as British Airways did at that time. I'm tee-total but was pleased to have a regular coffee. However, a group of young girls, by which I judged as probably in their early twenties, were knocking back glass after glass of free wine. After several being consumed in the first hour the head steward approached them with 'words of advice' and thereafter their consumption was rationed. Between coffees I was able to read, day dream and gaze out of the window. A meal was consumed and as we neared our destination the required landing card completed then, it seemed in no time at all, we were told to put on our seat belts and we landed smoothly at a sunny Moscow Domodedovo airport. With hand luggage only my disembarkation was easy. Following the signs with helpful English underneath I found border control, had my passport and visa checked and stamped, then into customs and I was through the process, back in Russia!

I stood on the airport concourse working out which way to head and eventually found the domestic flights wing of the building. Good. Then I located the British Airways desk and without problems managed to pick up my next boarding card for the flight to Rostov-on-Don, which was actually operated by Siberia Airlines. As I headed off for the domestic flights wing I realised that I would have to go through security again and instantly knew that my three bottles of water would not make it. I kicked myself for my ignorance but nevertheless checked with the uniformed lady officer at the security counter who indicated that I would need to drink them before going through. Finding a quiet corner I downed one bottle but was then at my limits. Seeing a couple of men waiting on seats nearby I gave the remaining two unopened bottles to them and headed off to security. This time there were no issues. My travel kettle element was spared and not queried.

Yet again I had a walk around and worked out the departure boards and what gate was where. As at Heathrow I had a couple of hours to wait but had a task to do before I sat and rested. Having got rid of my bottles of water before security I had to buy more now I was on the other side, given that bottled water is the only safe drinking water in Russia, and I still had a long journey ahead of me. I went into the airport kiosk and had a challenge. One crate of water bottles had light blue caps and one dark blue caps which I took to mean some were sparkling and some still water. However, which was which? With the help of a non-English speaking shop assistant and various bits of signing as well as some 'hissing' I successfully purchased the desired three bottles of still water. With that challenge mastered I bought a coffee, taking on trust that it was made with safe water, and then found a computer terminal and e-mailed home.

As I began to get tired and with time on my hands doubts began to creep into my mind as to whether I was doing the right thing going on a two week trip on my own. The call of the gate number meant I had to stop that train of thought and focus on the job in hand. I joined other passengers queuing for the transfer bus and chatted with some Germans who were commenting on my ukulele. When travelling alone even small snippets of conversation are an appreciated fillip and that was the case now. We boarded the plane, another Airbus I was pleased to note, even if painted a lurid bright green, and off we went, up and southwards towards Rostov-on-Don. I accepted that there would be no conversation with the incommunicative Russian lady next to me, the other seat being empty, although I did try. However, she did help me with the food options when these were announced.

The flight was uneventful, the landing greeted with clapping and we were decanted in the dark of night into the airport terminal. As I sipped from one of my bottles of water I showed my passport at border control again, went through the customs' green channel and looked around. There was a young lad holding a sign with just my name on it, and misspelt at that. That's when I knew I was on my own and the moment I really began to spiral downwards.

As is usual the airport was a distance out of the city and the taxi driver didn't speak English so it was a silent journey, just me and my thoughts. After driving through run down suburbs the taxi pulled up at the foot of the gangway to a large, white boat, with blue coloured trimmings and bright blue decks and, despite my research, much larger than I had expected. It must have been the length of a football pitch with three passenger decks, a sun deck and with portholes just above the waterline which I presumed was the crew accommodation. I already knew it had just over a hundred cabins and all in all it looked very smart and more like a floating hotel. It was rather intimidating.

The taxi driver wanted to carry my bags for me, I suspected for a tip, but I was well able to carry my own luggage so took the bags off him and headed on board into a carpeted reception area with a pair of spiral staircases with glazed balustrades, one on each side, and manned by two smartly dressed girls. By this time I was weary and low, probably due to tiredness and I was becoming mentally 'wobbly'. The receptionists smiled kindly and were very pleasant. They took my passport to photocopy, which I retrieved the next day, ticked me off a list, and gave me a leaflet giving the layout of the boat and joining instructions together with the itinerary for the following day, similar versions of which would appear each day thereafter, slipped under my cabin door. I was handed a cabin key with strict instructions to return it to the pigeon hole behind the reception desk whenever I left the boat and I was told that I was in Group 5, led by a Katya, with a tour of Rostov-on-Don starting the next day at 9am. Thanking the receptionists for all of this I asked if there was anywhere I could get a bite to eat and was told, apologetically, that I had missed dinner and there was no food available, even though a late dinner for JGR arrivals was listed on the joining instructions.

So there I was, tired, hungry, mentally vulnerable and suddenly feeling a very long way from home. Oh dear. However, it was at that moment that a man, another passenger, appeared and handed in his key to go out and, most importantly, he was British! I was so appreciative of hearing English spoken by a native of the UK that I exclaimed to him 'You're English?' and he looked surprised, as anyone would, but after a day of hearing mostly foreign voices it was a real joy to find that there were other Brits on board. I would soon find out that there was actually a SAGA party on the trip and they were a joyful, good-natured bunch.

Looking at the plan of the boat I climbed the spiral stairs up to the next level and arrived at my nice but slightly claustrophobic and airless cabin. This had red curtains at the window overlooking the deck, of which only the top fanlight opened, with orange walls of thin construction and not sound proof and a blue carpet, sapele doors and a mustard coloured plastic toilet and shower pod with a small wash basin and a door, the reverse of which had a sign warning not to put paper down the toilet since this was vacuum operated and paper would block the system. I would need to get used to that. The room was furnished with two beds which would fold back against the wall, as well as a shelf and hanging space.

I looked around despondently. The cabin was sufficient in itself but I immediately decided that this was not where I would spend my time. The cabin would be for sleeping only. Every other second of the day would be spent elsewhere.

All of my anxiety trigger points were being pressed and I did an audit of my situation. I was tired, mentally weak and with only two bottles of water remaining together with a packet of biscuits brought from home, all of that to last until breakfast time. If the trip was going to be like this I wouldn't survive and I honestly thought I would be quickly heading back home. Maybe a two week trip such as this was beyond me. By now it was gone ten o'clock with the darkness of night setting in. However, I decided to go for a walk along the narrow brick paved dockside where I had seen some kiosks and where party-type music was playing. As I handed in my cabin key to reception I heard a familiar voice and was face to face with one of the Germans who had commented on my ukulele at the airport. That was a genuinely real boost to my spirits.

I couldn't really work out the dockside. It seemed to be a social scene with courting couples, karaoke and with party boats on the river which at this point was about three times as wide as the Thames in central London. I wandered for a little while and then headed back and asked reception if there was a computer from which I could send an e-mail home and was told 'nyet', no, and when I asked about bottles of water I was told I could purchase those from the bar. I did but at an exorbitant price. At that point I gave up, returned to my cabin, drank another bottle of water and ate my biscuits, sent a text message home which was thankfully quickly answered, set my alarm to get an early start tomorrow and then went to bed and found the relief of sleep.

PROGRESS UP THE DON

TOMORROW IS ALWAYS ANOTHER day and it was and this time much, much better. I slept well, thankfully only woke up a couple of times and even then was able to successfully drift back to sleep. Dawn on Tuesday 1st May - May Day - arrived. It seemed so much longer than a day since I had left home and I had hardly thought of work at all - I had been too occupied with the effort of travelling! I got up and dressed early, finished off my water, handed in my key at reception and walked along the river front in the cool, clear morning air which foretold a hot day to come, watching as I went the myriad fishermen with their various rods and lines in the river and the street cleaners with their birch twig brooms and also looking at statues in the green set behind the trees lining the dockside as well as at the Soviet emblems on the roofs of some of the nearby tall office blocks.

After half an hour or so I went back, collected my key and explored the boat - the lounge area, the open outside decks, the small shop and the so-called 'library', actually just a few shelves of books in various languages in a space in the bow that couldn't be used for anything else. Importantly I found the dining room where breakfast would be served. As the serving time of seven o'clock approached a small crowd started to form outside the dining room doors which were opened on time to reveal a sumptuous spread of cooked meats, yoghurts, fruit juices, cereals and pastries, tea and coffee, all set out buffet style. That suited me well and after taking a suitable selection of food I was able to share a table with Hanse and Nete, a Dutch couple from Utrecht. They were good conversationalists, spoke excellent English, as is the case with nearly all Dutchmen, and had flown to Rostov-on-Don through Vienna in only four hours! I was jealous. They thought that there were two or three other Brits on the boat but most of the passengers they had met were German. The quality of the breakfast was good. The quantity was eye watering. Someone who knows these things later told me that people can put on a pound of weight a day on a cruise and I can easily see why. However, that day quality and quantity were what I needed and with a full stomach and pleasant breakfast company I felt a lot better and my mental state improved.

At the end of breakfast the boat shop was opened and I purchased a few postcards to write and send home. The young female shop assistant manning the till asked whether I was going to pay in dollars or euros and was flummoxed when I suggested roubles. She had to go away and work out the price. What I thought of as a given - that in Russia you need roubles - obviously wasn't the case. Instead, the boat was fully geared up for tourists. I walked away to the top sun deck with my postcards and an amused smile and sat and read for a while, enjoying the warmth of the sun's rays.

The itinerary had told me that there was a tour of Rostov-on-Don that morning so shortly before the appointed time of 9am I went to the reception area where other passengers were also assembling and looked for someone official-looking waving a number five. In the end I saw a wand with '5' at its head down on the quayside where a row of modern coaches was parked and I would find that all the coaches used in the various cities and towns we visited would be modern, with one exception. Key handed in I headed towards the wand and so met my guardian for the next two weeks. Katya was tall, efficient, helpful and spoke good English. Some coaches had only Germans, I believe the SAGA group had a coach to themselves and the coach for Group 5 had all the 'leftovers' - an assortment of English speakers including Swiss, Australians, a couple of New Zealanders, an American couple and several Dutch. We filed on board and were counted like school children on a trip. I would get used to that but we were never told to line up in pairs and hold hands! I found out later that if someone got left behind the group leader would have to remain and find them and then work out how to catch up with the boat, whether by train or taxi, at its next port.

The coach moved off into the city which is a fairly young metropolis, having been founded in 1749. It is situated mainly on the north bank of the Don River and is not to be confused with Rostov-Veliky which is north-east of Moscow. The city was ninety per cent destroyed in the Second World War, when it was occupied twice by the Germans, so is actually of modern construction. Its population now is about 1.1 million.

I found that the city improved and the streets became tree lined as the coach progressed uphill away from the run-down dock area and the river. The tour guide on the coach, Ylena, spoke into a microphone explaining the history and various sights. Many roads were closed for the May Day public holiday festivities which coincided with the celebrations of the seventy-fifth anniversary of Rostov becoming a region. The coach parked up and we were taken on foot to Theatre Square in the Armenian Quarter with its holiday crowds, bright flag display and a tall, needle-thin monument and where a group of school children were performing a dance routine on a raised platform with a Red Bull blow up arch nearby. I admired the concrete Soviet sculptures on the town hall behind the stage. From there we were led around the local area and shown a civil war statue and also a statue of the Russian hero Alexander Nevsky outside a newly built church on the site of a former Soviet square. However, generally there were few churches but parks were abundant.

One of the joys of travelling is meeting others and learning from them. I got chatting with other passengers as we walked around including an Australian man, Neville, with his Russian wife, Galina, who originated in this Rostov and who had together recently spent two weeks in London. Another couple, Dutch this time from Delft, always carried, whenever they travelled, some Delft china shoes to give away to staff. What a nice idea I thought. They then promptly pressed one into my hand and insisted I take it. All these years later I still have it. At one point I strolled along with the tour guide and she explained that she had always lived in the Rostov region and learned her excellent English at school and college. Katya had learned hers at school as well as some German and spent a year in Colorado and had recently spent two weeks in London. She thought that London Underground trains were wonderful!

Ylena took us to the memorial to the thirty thousand Jews who were marched out of the city by the Germans in the Second World War and executed and this was very moving with its summer-only guard of uniformed secondary school students, apparently always the top straight A grade students. I asked Katya how Russians view the Germans now and can they forgive them? Her reply was very gracious - 'not all Germans were Nazis then and now the Germans are a different generation'. She felt sorry for those Germans who still felt guilty at what had been done. I was humbled by her answers.

Before we got back on the coach I bought a one litre bottle of water for a fraction of the price I paid at the boat's bar. Counted, coached back to the boat and re-embarked we were now ready for departure. There was a large crowd on the dockside waving the boat off with music playing through the boat's loud speakers and it was quite a celebration due to Rostov being the boat's home port where most of the crew originated. As we moved into midstream and sailed up the tree lined Don towards our first stop on the tour, Starocherkassk, we were one of several boats heading the same way, all in procession and there were not only tourist boats but many cargo vessels as well.

Lunch was served at half past twelve as we travelled. Tables were assigned. My dining companions were Peter and Rosemary, a couple in their fifties who were travelling with JGR as well and we were the only three JGR passengers on the boat. They had unusual careers. Peter was a government scientist specialising in all things bread and Rosemary managed a crematorium. I found out later that Peter was due to pick up an Honorary Doctorate from a Hungarian university for his work. They had travelled to Burma, Indochina, Yeman and in Russia had journeyed up the Yenesei river. I felt very much the amateur but Peter and Rosemary were unpretentious and were really good company throughout the trip. Their adult daughter had the travel bug as well they said but it had passed by their son who was an accountant. I was pleased to learn that my meals throughout the trip would be shared with them. This lunch meal was again huge and I resolved to maybe miss future lunches and only have two meals a day. After the meal and every meal the staff came round offering shots of vodka, chargeable to the bar tab. I declined these. After a lemonade with this first meal, also chargeable to the bar tab, I stuck to water, surprisingly not provided as part of the lunch but only from my own supplies.

As soon as I could I went out onto the top sun deck with its tables, chairs and loungers to see what was going on. Contrary to my initial view that most passengers were older than me I did see that there were many younger people as well. I wasn't there long before the boat docked at Starocherkassk, Old Cherkassk, a Cossack village. This once fortified settlement on the north bank of the Don had been a town and was founded, on a flood plain, in 1593. It was the Don Cossack capital until the late eighteenth century. As such it had a population in the region of twenty thousand people. However, the Czar, Alexander I, forced the capital to relocate to Novocherkassk, New Cherkassk, and the once bustling town declined and is now little more than a farming village.

We walked from the boat into the village in our groups, being frequently counted, each group with its own local guide, the name of whom for Group 5 I did not catch. We stood by the outside wall of a building with a painting of a Cossack man, naked but still holding his gun, and were told how this was used as a Cossack motif after Peter the Great had admired a drunk Cossack in that very situation.

We wandered through the village with its prominent above ground yellow painted gas pipework and its well-kept wreath-covered war memorial until we came to the early eighteenth century green roofed and eight onion domed Cathedral of Christ's Resurrection with a huge separate bell tower and with black robed and bearded priests. At this point the ladies in the group had to put on head scarves before entering inside the church. I watched as the local Russians, as well as those from the boat, crossed themselves and bowed. Moving on from there we were taken to a compound and had an entertainment in the Hetman's - Headman's - house with a group of locals singing traditional Cossack songs and dancing. However, when spectators started to be pulled off the bench seats onto the dance floor I slipped out and admired the building instead with its brick ground floor walls, built to withstand flooding from the Don, and similar to many other buildings in the village, and its timber framed upper walls. The singing and dancing entertainment over the group wandered back to the boat and as we did so I took the opportunity to buy another good-sized bottle of drinking water from a kiosk on the way.

A little while later, as the boat moved off again into mid-stream, I could see from the sun deck the flatness of the land, the view broken by the top of the occasional distant but still prominent church serving some hidden village. Loaded bulk cargo carriers with raised bridges at the rear motored past, heading south. I sat on this deck watching the world go by, finding the motion of the boat much smoother than the Trans-Siberian train had been on my previous adventure. I gazed at the locals stretched out relaxing in the sunshine or fishing at the many beaches we passed. I too relaxed.

Towards the end of the afternoon a required emergency evacuation drill was held. Everyone had to go to their cabins, wait for the alarm bell and then put on the life jackets kept in the cabins and head out into the corridor and thence to the relevant life boat station. As we did this crew members took photographs of us. It was during this exercise that I discovered that the unknown button in my cabin operated the boat PA system since initially I didn't hear the alarm sound in my room and had to look for a volume control. The exercise took about thirty minutes and instead of leaving me reassured that we would survive any sinking of the boat it made me think that the whole exercise showed we would all struggle to get out in time!

I returned to the upper deck and started writing out in Russian, which I didn't and still don't know, but in which I was aided by a phrase book and an English/Russian dictionary, simple phrases to put on my postcards home. I could have gone to the Captain's Welcome Reception but why? I had come to see Russia, not the inside of the boat's lounge. I was happy to stay where I was. Dinner came and went with too much food and with good conversation with Peter and Rosemary including descriptions of Peter's bread hunting exploits and mill tours in foreign lands, finding out and advising the government on the most productive types of wheat for given situations. His expertise in bread put him in a different league to even the most skilled baker! Vodka was again offered - and declined - but I was again surprised that no water was provided with the meal.

As we journeyed into the evening the boat traffic became less and less with only the occasional small boat nearby and with the countryside more and more deserted except for lone fishermen. My first instinct was that the Russians fished as a sport but I do wonder now, on reflection, whether there was an element also of catching a meal. Either way, the Russians - or at least Russian men - love to fish.

The evening was spent on the sun deck reading, continuing with my postcard phrases and gazing at the passing countryside although I did take some time out from that to listen to some live music from the boat's band in the lounge. I stayed outside until dusk came and night fell, only going back to my cabin to make myself a coffee with my kettle element which I then took outside, careful not to spill any, to enjoy in the cool air.

Already the stresses of home and work were fading and I turned in feeling relaxed and free of anxiety about the trip and everything else in life. With the gentle, steady rocking motion of the boat I quickly slipped into a deep sleep although I was aware of the boat bumping against the wall of a lock at some point.

Nevertheless, I awoke on the Wednesday feeling nervy and

anxious. That may have had something to do with the wake-up music played through the cabin speaker but turning that off sorted that out! I got up, cleared my things into my bag - the previous day I had returned to my cabin to find that the cleaner had carefully folded up my slightly scruffy pyjamas and put them on the pillow, which I thought was a personal service too far - then sent a text home but only really calmed when I was able to share breakfast with an older retired English couple, John and Wendy, part of the SAGA party which apparently was about twenty-five strong. They were in a group all of their own for the off-boat tours and had a Russian speaking SAGA escort with them who, apparently, was about seventy-five years old, had family in England and was British but lived in Russia and was bilingual and had been an escort for many years and knew several of the local tour guides. However, at some point on the trip he caught a bug and was confined to his cabin for several days with his meals taken to his cabin door.

My breakfast companions spoke about travel which is always a good subject with which to open a conversation. Their travel experiences had taken them on the Silk Road by train from Uzbekistan through Kazakhstan to China in the mid-1990s and also touring in Africa, South America and elsewhere. Each such conversation put seeds into my mind as to future possibilities. Their family, children and grandchildren, were spread across the United Kingdom and the USA. I appreciated the company, the conversation and the social contact which were all good for my mental well-being although the gentleman was inclined to be pompous and put his wife down. As the trip went on I observed the group dynamics and this man along with others seemed to enjoy the cruise experience and was not too interested in what was happening outside the boat whereas other passengers, Peter and me included, would happily skip a meal to see outside.

This day was a cruising day with no shore landings at all. After breakfast I made the decision to abandon the sun deck which was very hot, in fact too hot, due to its lack of shade and did not have much conversation, although there was the occasion exchange with some of the German passengers. Instead, I found a home on the more intimate walk around deck below which had more shade from the sun beneath the overhanging deck above and also, I found, had more opportunity for conversation when sitting at one of the scattered tables there.

As I sat there we came to another lock. This was large with concrete side walls and towers at each end topped with statues and with arches spanning between these over the lock and with ornate lamps on the quaysides. Flashing traffic lights controlled the entry and exit of boats. The boat only just fitted with about two foot - sixty centimeters - of clearance each side and with crew members on deck calling directions to the bridge. All such boats traversing the locks must have a similar issue and also must be of shallow draft. Interestingly, whilst most locks had conventional door type gates some had gates that rose up vertically through the water on a chain drive. It was an efficient operation, watched over by pretty female soldiers carrying very big machine guns. Welcome to Russia! However, I presumed that was due to the relative proximity of this area to the troubled Chechnya and Dagestan regions. More locks followed.

On the other side of the locks the boat entered the wide expanse of the Tsimyansk reservoir, passing an elegant rostral column as it did so.

With no landings I had a sedentary day ahead of me so took time out from reading and day dreaming to go to a Russian language class run by Katya. That was a difficult and humbling experience. The most important thing I learned at the class was that I am not a linguist but I was glad I had tried. Instead of practicing speaking Russian I spent the time after class and before lunch focused on completing my Russian phrases for my postcards and then went and found Katya. She kindly checked and corrected my attempts so I could then copy the phrases out. I was very satisfied with my two whole sentences of Russian written on each card! At the shop I paid for postage and was told that at the next stop, Volgograd the next day, a crew member would take them to the post office. I wasn't at all sure they would get home before me and in fact they didn't but it's the thought that counts.

I found a seat in the shade at a table at the stern and checked our progress on my map, read, gazed at the scenery and watched the swallows following the boat.

Lunchtime came and as we trouped into the dining room the photographs taken during the previous day's emergency drill were pinned up on the information board for people to purchase. Personally, I would have paid to have mine destroyed and looking at the others the quality was no better. At least it was nice not to be alone in the bad photo stakes. Aware of my waistline I only had the main course of lunch and skipped the starter and dessert for the outside air.

On a sailing day such as this, as well as language classes, the boat offered a Russian dancing class, a film, 'Russia - the Land of the Czars Part I', and a presentation by the gift shop on 'Russian Painting and Applied Arts History'. I was tempted by some of these but definitely not the dancing. However, in the end I relaxed outside and watched the world go by, waiting patiently and contentedly for the next major event which was the evening meal. Whilst doing so I admired the reservoir running without interruption to the horizon with no shore line even visible.

When the evening meal came it had a sea food starter but knowing the reputation of sea food for poisoning, causing upset stomachs, I declined mine, as did Peter and Rosemary. The main course came and was enjoyed but that was as far as the meal went. It was disturbed by the boat entering a lock. As with the first locks I found this very exciting, as did Peter, and we could not restrain ourselves and left poor Rosemary at the table and headed out to watch what was going on. A further lock quickly followed and these marked the start of the Lenin Volga-Don Shipping Canal.

This canal is a major engineering achievement at the closest convergence of the Don and Volga rivers. In times past the Vikings used to carry their boats between these rivers, using the lakes in between to assist. The Ottomans started a canal in the sixteenth century but did not complete it. Peter the Great tried to build a canal in the seventeenth century but failed to make progress. It was only after the Second World War that the one hundred and one kilometer route was successfully canalled, with the use of German prisoners of war, although forty-five kilometers is through lakes and reservoirs. As ever on the major Soviet construction projects at that time conditions were harsh and German prisoners of war considered expendable and the death rate was high. Nevertheless, along with the presence of other canals in northern Russia a north-south trade route was eased.

Peter and I eventually returned to the very understanding and tolerant Rosemary, still waiting at the dining table, and the meal was completed. Before we left the table Katya came round collecting the entrance fee for the optional visit to the panorama exhibition in Volgograd the next day, which I gladly paid.

Refreshed by the dinner I headed back out on deck as soon as possible to see the boat traverse the canal, although I did wander back inside to listen to the boat band for a time.

The boat reached another lock and I watched as it manoeuvred through this. I was not the only passenger observing this operation and we all chatted together. It was an opportunity to meet another couple in the SAGA party, this time from Portishead overlooking the Bristol Channel. There were fewer spectators now and gradually, as darkness fell, more and more people slipped away to their cabins. I knew I couldn't stay there all night and so eventually I too went to my cabin and slept, knowing that the next day, Thursday, we would reach the mighty Volga!

NORTH ON THE VOLGA

WHEN I AWOKE ON Thursday we were still in the Lenin canal but during the night had passed through several more locks. I caught sight of one of these as I had a pre-breakfast stroll on deck, avoiding the passengers doing their organised morning stretching exercises, an event that happened at the start of each day. My stroll completed I headed for breakfast to get that finished before the boat reached the final locks descending into the Volga, the river referred to by Russians as Dear Mother Volga.

Breakfast was enjoyable. I shared a table with a Latvian couple of Russian descent, Irina, for whom this was a birthday treat, her actual birthday being the next day, and her husband Igor as well as her mother Margareta. Irina was the only one who spoke a little English and she explained that this was their second cruise, having a couple of years ago been on the Nile. After breakfast I went to my now usual deck and watched the boat manoeuvre through the last of the locks, past a statue of Lenin and a type of rostral column with a further columned feature at its head, and finally progress out into the Volga, a wide, wide, wide river, so, so much wider than the Don. An unidentified writer once said 'The Volga is Russia herself - her people, her history, her nature' and we were there. We had arrived.

As we chugged slowly up river, following another cruise boat, I skipped the Russian Songs Class - I'm not sure I would ever have gone - and instead watched the extensive and ugly sprawling mass of Volgograd come into sight on the western river bank. This city was founded in 1589 where the Tsaritsa river joins the Volga and until the 1920s was called Tsaritsyn. It then became known as Stalingrad. Stalin fought there in the Russian civil war and in the 1920s and 1930s it became a major industrial centre. As Stalingrad it became famous for its siege by the German army in 1942 and the Soviet counter-siege in 1943. With the disgrace of Stalin the name of the city was changed again, in 1961, to become

Volgograd. As well as a Russian population the city used to have a longstanding population of German descent dating from the later eighteenth century and the time of Catherine the Great who, after conquering the southern Volga region, needed to populate the area. She turned to Germany for immigrants and these were happy to come and kept their culture, language, traditions and churches but their ancestry proved disastrous for them in the Second World War when they were deported eastwards by Stalin.

Things on the boat moved so slowly that there was time for an early lunch before the boat got to the Volgograd river port, although I restricted myself to only a starter. Outside on deck again I saw that we were waiting for the cruise boat ahead of us to dock before we did and that was frustrating but a queue is a queue and we would have to wait our turn. That eventually came at about half past twelve and everyone started gathering in reception to hand in their keys ready for disembarkation onto the fleet of coaches waiting on the shore road between the river port and the steep escarpment on the other side. Sadly this escarpment hid the city from immediate view, although, making me envious, Peter managed to cross the very busy road and run up the escarpment steps to have a quick look at the city from the top. I tried to follow him but the road was too busy for me to manage. Stepping out in front of speeding cars trusting that they will stop was beyond my courage! Loaded onto the right coach, having followed the '5' wand waved by Katya, and having been counted several times, we set off for a city tour.

Volgograd is defined by its role in the Second World War. We got off the coach first at the Avenue of Heroes, which is actually a square but with two rows of Russian flags and a monument at the end of these. The tour guide, Valentina, showed us the building on the corner of the square from which the German Commander, General Paulus, surrendered. We were given a short time to stroll around the area and then, seeing a nearby kiosk, I seized the moment and restocked my water supply with a large bottle before we were then summoned back to the coach. With us all returned onto that the driver Andrei took us towards the next stop while Valentina explained that the city was ninety per cent destroyed in the Second World War and serious consideration was given to leaving the whole city in that condition as a memorial and building a new city on a site elsewhere. However, this was eventually rejected in favour of rebuilding.

We were taken to the Bread Factory, one building of which has been left as a memorial in its battered war condition with no roof and every door and window opening destroyed. The Panorama Museum showing the battle is on this site and after viewing that we moved on to Mamayev Kurgan. This is a huge Tatar burial mound dating from the early fourteenth century which dominates the landscape and therefore became the scene of the most bitter war time fighting. It changed hands between the Soviets and the Germans many times. On top of the mound now is the enormous statue entitled The Motherland Calls, a one hundred and fifty two meter high representation of a winged lady shouting out whilst wielding a big sword. In contrast to the statue we entered the quiet and still of the remembrance hall, with its memorial flame coming from a torch held by a hand emerging from the floor and guarded by armed soldiers, before then approaching the Motherland statue through an avenue lined with red and yellow flags and with concrete sculpted battle scenes. All of this was very moving and the memorial is a UNESCO World Heritage site.

After climbing up the mound to the foot of the statue I sat quietly on my own gazing across the city until a group of Russian teenagers tried to engage me in conversation. This was a hopeless exercise, me with no Russian, them with no English, and we smiled at each other, shrugged shoulders and parted company. As with any tourist attraction the scammers were out trying to get tourists to buy something but noting the cost of just one postcard, on sale for what I thought was a huge amount, and comparing with the price I paid on the boat, which was probably at a high price, I was not at all tempted. After a while Katya collected us all back together to lead us to the coach where we were counted again before being taken back to the boat.

Dinner was an opportunity to relax and it was during this that the boat moved off from Volgograd and turned north. During the meal Katya asked to borrow my JGR itinerary since there seemed to be some discrepancy between the different groups as to which towns and cities were to be visited. She returned this later and any issue seemed to be resolved and certainly no cities listed on my itinerary were missed but I think that other groups had stops added since Kostroma, on my list, was not on the boat's circulated list of stops.

Immediately after dinner I watched our progress through a lock at a hydro-electric dam spanning the river just north of Volgograd and then sat again on my now favourite deck with my nose stuck into a book. People seemed to drop into predictable after dinner routines and I was now becoming aware of those. Some would go to the lounge, some to the bar, some to bed, some sat on deck and one couple seemed to spend each evening marching round and round the outside walkway, presumably as a keep fit routine. I remained seated and read but broke this to see the boat band with keyboard, accordion and a girl singer give another thoroughly enjoyable concert. Once that was over I sat outside again, watching the sun set across the water with the shoreline on the very horizon and tried to get to grips with basic Russian phrases but the Russian language is not at all easy.

Every day had so far been sunny from dawn to dusk and that was the case on Friday. I woke at dawn after an excellent night's sleep and as the boat sailed towards that day's stopover at the city of Saratov I collected my breakfast from the buffet and sat for a short while with a Russian mother and daughter who wondered whether I was American. Having revealed my true nationality to them and their breakfast finished I was left alone and resorted to my usual cover in such circumstances of reading, with a book always kept in my gilet pocket. When one is alone a book gives company, like a reliable friend. I was to find that my other reliable 'friend' would be my travel diary into which I entered not only a record of events but also anything I needed to remember as well as my deepest thoughts, hopes and fears. However, today a German couple from Dusseldorf soon joined me. This couple had cruised on the Anton Chekhov last year between Moscow and St Petersburg and were now completing the journey between north and south with this Volga adventure. They sorted out the German passengers for me, explaining that there were two parties of Germans with one of those parties also having some Austrians and Swiss.

Breakfast finished I was able to go almost immediately into the next Russian Language class held in the lounge, again by Katya. This was just as successful as the first class. After the class I absented myself from the lounge to avoid getting involved in a class on Russian dancing at which I would have been even more unsuccessful. The boat cruised up the river until, after lunch, I saw huge grain silos on the western river side indicating that our destination of Saratov had been reached. Again, though, we had to wait for a long time for a free berth to allow us to dock.

Saratov was founded in the late sixteenth century as a fortress town and later became a centre of population for the German immigrants under Catherine the Great. It is industrialised and currently has a population of approximately nine hundred thousand people.

Once the boat was safely berthed we were loaded onto coaches again and counted several times as the coach tour guide introduced herself as Natalya. We headed off and as we raced around the city were shown from the coach the various sights including the late seventeenth century Holy Trinity Cathedral, the large Orthodox seminary, which has a busy secular academic university side as well as a theological side, and the railway administration offices! Natalya explained that Saratov is famous for its manufacture of combine harvesters. There was a noticeable juxtaposition between the old timber clad buildings and modern glass covered structures and also noticeable was the absence of churches. I took this up with Natalya. 'Only five out of seventy churches', said Natalya, 'survived the revolution but there is now also a Roman Catholic church as well as two mosques.' The coach stopped in the main town square with its large statue of Lenin and colourfully decorated onion domes to the Church of the Icon of the Mother of God and we had a walk around. In particular I admired the mosaics rising to full multi-storey height on the end of tower blocks overlooking the area. We were led on from there to the hanger-like fruit and vegetable market with its steel truss roof and wandered through the separate aisles and into the various corners. That was when I had a fright.

I was busy admiring the brightly coloured and neatly displayed produce and on turning around to check where the rest of the group were I found that they weren't! There was no one I recognised in sight. I looked down the aisles. No one. I looked round corners. No one and at that point a wave of fear and panic swept through me. Even though I had a map of Saratov I had not been keeping track of where we were. I hadn't had the need to do so - all I had to do was follow Katya and her wand. Now I had no idea where I was relative to the river port and no idea what time the boat was due to depart. I was lost. I went to the market entrance where we had come in but nothing. Then I went to the other market entrance at the opposite end of the building and looked around. Extending from that entrance was a long pedestrianised street of shops which must have been the main retail centre and in the far distance I saw a couple of heads I recognised. Breathing a huge sigh of relief I rushed after them and lost no time at all in catching up with the party. They hadn't missed me and I didn't declare my near miss to them. Within the pedestrianised area was a McDonald's - I could read that name in Russian and, of course, the yellow arches were unmistakable - and I did feel the need for a take away coffee to help me recover and which I managed to order successfully in Russian, supported with a bit of sign language.

At the end of the pedestrianised area we got back onto the now waiting coaches, were counted a couple of times and then headed off and downhill towards the river. Before we got there we stopped again, trooped off the coach and went shopping in a small convenience store. Why I'm not sure and it must have been the store keeper's worst nightmare, having a coach load of foreign tourists invade his shop, all buying low value items in cash and needing change. All I bought was another bottle of water.

We rejoined the coach, were recounted and then taken to the port and re-embarked onto the boat. I joined the scramble at the reception desk and collected my cabin key and went to freshen up a bit and then stood outside to watch the boat's departure and admire the huge bridge over the Volga, three kilometers long and built in the 1960s.

During dinner that evening Katya came and collected the fee for tomorrow's optional excursion to Stalin's Bunker in the city of Samara. That, I thought, sounded really good and interesting and definitely not to be missed.

Later, after dinner, I again missed the film 'Russia - the Land of the Czars Part II' - and settled at a table on deck to read and view the scenery. A man came and sat the other side of the table and said something in German and when I apologised for not understanding he immediately switched to perfect English. I was very impressed and very ashamed at my own language skills. He introduced himself as Jim and came from Frankfurt where he worked as an optical engineer. We chatted for a long, long time about his country and the best places to stay, about economics, the EU, the environment and pleasantly on and on. The evening went quickly but in the end he made his way inside while I stayed where I was to watch the sun go down.

Another good night's sleep, so good that I was unaware of the lock we went through in the early hours, left me clear headed and alert for the next morning, Saturday. As each day passed the tensions from work were dissipating, my anxiety levels dropped and I could feel myself healing.

Feeling 'on the ball' on Saturday morning I sat again with the Russian mother and daughter I had met previously over breakfast but my attempt at saying 'good morning' in Russian was a disaster and came out as meaningless jabber. I accepted the inevitable and decided that I would never be a linguist. After they had finished their breakfast and slipped away I pulled out my book and read for a little while until a middle aged German, who introduced himself in good English as Reinhart from Berlin, joined me. I asked whether he learned his English at school but he said he was actually from East Germany and so as a child had learned Russian as his second language. He was a government research chemist, single and travelling alone and had also completed the Trans-Siberian Railway last year which gave us something in common. We talked about German language dialects and he told me that Germans from one area can have trouble understanding the accent of those from other parts of Germany, very similar to our English dialects. Before breakfast finished I had a chat with an English couple in the SAGA group, Roy and Edna, although Roy called her Delilah. As I have written before, these small snatches of conversation are a real lifeline when travelling alone.

I skipped the presentation on Icons and Lacquered Miniatures, given by the boat shop staff, and the Russian song class and the bingo and instead washed a couple of my shirts in the shower and hung them there to drip dry before reading and day dreaming on deck as before. Lunch came and went and it was not until mid-afternoon that the city of Samara came into view on the eastern river bank.

Samara was founded in 1586 at the confluence of the Volga and Samara rivers to defend the eastern frontier of Muscovy and protect the Volga trade route. It has been the centre of various upheavals including that of Stepin Razin in 1670 and Pugachev in 1774 and was seized by the Czechoslovak Legion in 1918 in the Russian Civil War. Originally it grew on the grain trade but is now also an industrial centre with a current population in the region of one million people.

As we approached the city the clear, pure countryside air we had enjoyed changed and areas of smog could be seen over industrial settlements so our first sight of Samara, even before the enormous thirteen span bridge over the river, was of the smoke pollution rising above the trees lining the river bank.

We docked, this time without any delay, and were herded onto our coaches, with those of us going to Stalin's Bunker given our own coach in charge of another crew member, the slightly built and petite terrier Natalya who waved the wand for us to follow. We had a city tour on board the coach, given by the coach's tour guide Alena including past the Soyuz rocket where we learned about the city's space industry. We stopped at the city square and disembarked. The square was being prepared for the ninth of May Victory Day celebrations, this being the big commemoration of the end of the Great Patriotic War, as the Russians call the Second World War. Parade rehearsals were taking place so we could not enter the square, which overlooked the river and had a very tall needle-thin statue topped by a figure, but could only see this from the perimeter. A nearby kiosk full of religious artifacts and icons drew my attention and I asked Alena the guide whether this was common to which she responded 'church is big business here'!

I referred to the group leader, Natalya, as a terrier. As we moved on from the city square she dealt very effectively and firmly with a car driver who had parked badly and blocked the coach and, much rebuked by a torrent of aggressive Russian from her, he swiftly moved and we were free to drive onto what appeared to be a residential estate of low rise flats where the coach parked. Leaving the coach we were taken into one of the ground floor homes from where we were led down, down and down lots and lots of stairs into Stalin's secret bunker. This had been built during the Great Patriotic War to give a command centre for Stalin should Moscow fall to the Germans and contained several decorated and furnished rooms which we were allowed to explore. However, Moscow did not fall to the Germans and it is not thought that Stalin ever visited the bunker. As we left the bunker a large squad of green uniformed soldiers was lining up, presumably practicing for the Victory Day celebrations.

Afterwards the coach, with its suitably counted occupants, headed back to the boat and I sat with German Jim, who was on the same bunker tour, and he and I had another chat. As we disembarked from the coach onto the dockside I thought I may have a few minutes to look more closely at a nearby church, only a hundred yards or so away. Katya would have let me. However, on telling Natalya my intentions she looked me in the eye and responded 'It may be better to get back on the boat'. Now that was not a suggestion but a command and with a big stick, the wand, in her hand and having seen the power of her mouth already I decided that it was wisest to do as she said!

Over dinner Peter, Rosemary and I reviewed the day and again avoided the starter which was star fish, small whole star fish, suckers and all. Outside the air temperature had fallen with our progress northwards but the skies were still clear so after dinner I spent a little while in the fresh air, then not feeling tired, I left the deck area and went into the library and browsed the books, went back to my cabin for a quiet ukulele strum and finally settled into bed just before midnight and fell straight asleep. I did not sleep for long. A little while after midnight I was woken by a bump to the boat and the noise of the engines revving. We had entered another lock so I quickly dressed and headed outside to see what was going on. The Anton Chekhov was the second boat into a huge lock and the crew were again showing great skill in manoeuvring the boat into the space available. The whole process of going through the lock was time consuming but fascinating and had to be repeated for a second lock. Eventually I collapsed back into bed in the early hours, very tired but relaxed and happy.

However, the following day, Sunday, my late night caught up with me and I lacked energy. My mood was not helped by the cold weather and overcast sky, nor by the earlier than normal breakfast, timed so we could dock in the next city, Ulyanovsk, to join the waiting coaches at 9am. It was definitely not helped either by the ugliness of Ulyanovsk.

This city was founded on the western river bank as a fortress in 1648, again to protect the borders of Muscovy, and was originally called Simbirsk. It was the birthplace of Vladimir Ilyich Ulyanov, better known as Lenin, after whom it was renamed, and interestingly also the birthplace of the man Lenin replaced, Alexander Kerensky. It is now an industrial centre as evidenced by the cranes at the dockside.

Katya was back in charge of our coach party. The local guide, Galina, was a university lecturer, with excellent English and presumably giving tours to earn extra income in his summer holidays. He had spent time in Bournemouth the year before. As we were driven around Ulyanovsk I saw nothing to particularly commend the city and our guide himself described the city as backward. We did get off the coach to visit a small museum dedicated to Lenin in the flat where he once lived and which was situated in a form of conservation area where old buildings were preserved. I didn't go in and was happy to do a walkabout on my own instead, seeing a German Lutheran church, unusual in an Orthodox country and a hint of the area's German heritage. A policeman was wandering about armed with a machine gun and there were a few street art statues. What was noticeable was the chirping of birds, which had been largely absent so far on our journey, as well as swarms of flies which also, thankfully, had been absent so far.

Back with the group and onto the coach we were taken to the main city square, with its 1970s flat roofed city hall, where I was able to buy some more water as well as a refreshing ice cream. A visit to the city museum followed.

As the coach returned us to the river port the guide Galina gave us a parting thought saying 'Some of our history may be bad but if we have no history then we have no future'. I found that very profound.

Now on the boat, which remained moored for some hours more, I had my usual light lunch, during which Katya came round offering those who were willing a tour of the boat's bridge and asking that we book that at the reception desk. Needless to say, straight after the meal I booked.

Later, while still in the river port the time came to leave the outside deck and assemble in reception for the bridge tour. This was fascinating and included a question and answer session. As we left the bridge I made a light hearted comment to Katya that the bridge tour was really good but seeing the engine room would be exciting. She just smiled back at me.

We eventually cast off from ugly, grey Ulyanovsk and I sat at my usual table outside, watching the world go by and noticing that we were in the company of another cruise boat, the Rachmaninov. As I relaxed I turned my thoughts to the next day when we were due at last into Kazan, the one city of all others that I wanted to see.

The evening meal came and went. Katya came round to collect an entrance fee from those who wished to visit the Raifa Monastery in Kazan but I decided to opt out of that since other plans were forming in my mind. Dinner was followed later in the evening by a concert by the boat's musicians entitled 'Russian Romance' for which I slipped into the back of the lounge to hear.

Before settling down for the night I checked my map and made the judgment that the boat would not be at Kazan until well after sunrise which would be at around a quarter to five in the morning. I had hoped to see the sun rise in Kazan a second time and it was a huge shame that that would not happen but there was nothing I could do about it. Nevertheless, I was up at 6am the next day, Monday, to see the boat sail beneath the long, steel girdered bridges across the Volga and in expectation of our arrival at Kazan river port.

KAZAN AND BEYOND

KAZAN IS A CITY that predates the rise of Muscovy, being founded by the Bulgars on the eastern bank of the Volga in around the year 1000. It was subjugated by the Tatar Mongols but became an independent khanate in 1438. Subsequently it was conquered by Ivan the Terrible in 1552 allowing Muscovy to expand eastwards. Ivan the Terrible banished the Tatars to the northern side of the Bulak Canal which runs through the city and the effects of that are still felt today with the city divided on that line between Orthodox Russians and the Muslim Tatars. It is a university city with alumni including Tolstoi and Lenin and was the scene of a key communist victory in the Russian civil war.

Frustratingly, as we approached the city, both the Rachmaninov, which was in the lead, and the Anton Chekhov sat outside the river port for well over an hour, probably waiting for a berth. As the boats waited a storm swept over us, full of sleet, torrential rain and fork lightning so I retreated inside for breakfast in the company of the Australian Neville, with whom I had chatted on the first day, and his wife Galina. However, as soon as possible I went back outside to watch the boat dock near to the modern, fully glazed port building. This time we had to moor on the outside of the Rachmaninov. The reception areas of the respective boats were aligned allowing us to walk through the Rachmaninov to get ashore. The advantage of that arrangement was that, when we came to leave, the Anton Chekhov would be first away.

By the time we eventually landed it had stopped raining but showers would continue on and off all morning and umbrellas had to be frequently put up. I discovered then that my waterproofs were too heavy and really meant for severe weather and were clumsy to put on and wear. I resolved to change those if I ever did another journey. Nevertheless, it did become really hot as the day went on and the afternoon was dry. After landing we were assembled as usual at our coaches, with those for the Raifa Monastery in a separate coach. With Katya in the lead we boarded, were counted and then, as we moved off, were introduced to our driver Sergei and the city tour guide, Irina, who took us past the Lenin statue in the city square to the early eighteenth century Orthodox Cathedral of Saints Peter and Paul. This had an ornately decorated tiered tower and a huge neon sign inside proclaiming 'Christ is Risen' above the sanctuary screen, very out of keeping with the cathedral's old and ornate decorations. Many black dressed nuns rather than priests were wandering around and all the Russians, including the young, were bowing and scraping in front of the sanctuary screen and at various icons. Apparently, the services are in old Russian which not all Russians nowadays can understand. Then it was on to the Kremlin complex with its extensive white perimeter walls and conical headed towers and a leaning fifty nine meter high brick-finished tower adjacent to the white painted onion domed Annunciation Cathedral, both built in the 1550s.

After the churches we went to the nearby blue roofed mosque on the same site, blue tipped minarets pointing skywards from each corner, newly built with the benefit of Saudi Arabian money and which was opened only about seven years previously. Compared to the highly decorated Orthodox churches the mosque was very unadorned and light and airy with plain undecorated walls but decorative tiled floors, decorated balustrades and a patterned dome ceiling.

This mix of Christian and Islamic places of worship in the Kremlin reflects the religions and the cultures of the local people living side by side in the city. I noticed the bilingual signs and the tour guide explained that the Tatar language has an additional six letters when compared with the thirty-three letter Cyrillic alphabet. She said that the different ethnic groups live reasonably happily alongside each other with she herself having a Ukrainian mother but a Tatar father.

As we moved around as a group we chatted to each other and

to Katya as well as other Russian staff on the trip. Katya revealed that the cruise was her summer holiday and that her full time job was in an office in Rostov, where our trip started. She would love to visit Lake Baikal and Vladivostok but for her it was cheaper to get to South Africa than places such as those at the other end of Russia. I realised then that I had probably seen more of Russia than the average Russian citizen. Our conversations covered all sorts of areas and I gained a fascinating insight into Russian life. One of the Russian staff perceptively commented that he thought democracy had probably gone as far as it would in Russia. As I write this in 2023 I realise how little then did he know the truth of that!

The city tour finished and the group assembled by the coaches to be bussed back to the river port for lunch. However, with several hours to spare before departure I had an opportunity. I had a conversation with the ever-shepherding Katya who insisted we exchange mobile numbers and then, with map in hand and strict instructions from Katya not to get lost, I was free to go walkabout! I felt so brave.

That day was a public holiday for Inauguration Day - the inauguration for the third time of Vladimir Putin as President of Russia - and so the streets were crowded with locals relaxing and shopping as well as lots of tour groups with their minders, cameras and back packs, just like us. As I headed off I watched with interest as a trolley bus driver engaged the bus pick up with a wooden stick. I walked through the pedestrianised main street with its lady balancing white doves on her arms and its static processional coach and cat street statues and coming across a McDonald's I managed to successfully buy a coffee and a milkshake. I went to a supermarket and followed everyone else in putting my backpack containing waterproofs, umbrella, reading book and water bottle into a locker before entry, something which is not done in the United Kingdom but is, I found out, very routine in Russia. There I bought myself an ice cream, a bottle of Coca Cola and a two litre bottle of water.

For the rest of the time I just walked, explored and observed the city and its numerous street statues. There was a noticeable lack of timber buildings here and a huge amount of construction work and many newly finished buildings including the elegant classical columned government building with a nearby life size horse and cart street statue. All of this showed the region's prosperity which was from the drilling of oil. However, the pavements were extremely uneven and had to be used with considerable care, and the rails on which the trams ran had huge potholes beneath them in some locations and flexed significantly although the trams, whilst wobbling across these, stayed upright and continued running.

As I wandered and went to cross a road I suddenly heard the screech of tyres and a car sped round a corner on the other carriageway from me and then crashed in to a row of parked vehicles! Several concerned people rushed towards it and it appeared that the elderly gentleman driver had just lost control. He was badly shaken but otherwise unhurt, unlike the cars he had hit. I was very relieved that I hadn't tried to cross the road seconds earlier otherwise I would have been right in the way. As a tourist it was not for me to get involved, even as a witness, so I moved on.

I went around a few poorer side streets with small local mosques and plain unadorned buildings and then, following my map, I headed for the river bank and strolled along the Volga embankment. I had got really hot during my walkabout and arrived back at the boat in desperate need of a shower which I went and had. Later, clean and refreshed and making sure that Katya knew I was back, I went out again, this time only strolling along the river bank as far as the train station before returning, watching the fishermen trying for a catch as I went. With a coffee in my hand I sat on deck and read and then, as we eventually departed, watched and gazed at the city with its captivating skyline of churches and mosques.

As we moved out into mid-stream dinner was served,

accompanied by a firework display on shore, presumably in connection with Inauguration Day. After I had eaten and the meal was finished I sat on the stern of the boat with the upper deck above providing some shelter from the evening sun. A husband and wife joined me and we got chatting but I could not quite place where they were from. We played a guessing game for a while but in the end they had to help me and proclaimed themselves as Gibraltarians which I would never have thought of. They were bilingual in English and Spanish and had booked the trip as part of a Spanish group from the Madrid area. They were very happy to be British and did not want to join with Spain. In a conversation with the lady a few days later she explained how much they objected to Spanish workers, who had been shut out of Gibraltar by their own government, now, with the border reopened, expecting to take the place of the Moroccans who had filled the vacancies their absence had left. We talked for a long time, watching the scenery and islands with derelict abandoned forts go by as well as observing gas flares from oil wells in the distance and avoiding the showing of the film 'Russia - the Land of the Czars Part III'. After the couple turned in I continued to sit until the sun went down and it got dark.

Refreshed by a good night's sleep, again missing a lock in the early hours, I enjoyed breakfast on Tuesday morning with a half deaf American from California as well as a German man and, after they had departed, with Hanse and Nete, the Dutch couple I had eaten breakfast with on the very first day. They had gone to the monastery tour the previous day and had found it disappointing so I was glad I had turned that down. They enjoyed cruising though and had previously cruised both the Nile and in Italy.

This day the boat was making two city stops, firstly at Cheboksary and later in the day at Kosmodemyansk. The sky was clear and the temperature warm as we approached Cheboksary and the view of the city, with green and blue roofed churches to the fore as the boat went into the river port, was picturesque.

Cheboksary is the capital of the Chuvash Republic of Russia

and is located on the south bank of the Volga, the river having now turned towards Moscow. It was originally a Bulgar city, founded in the thirteenth century, in an agricultural area. It became part of Muscovy in 1555 at which time a frontier fortress was built. The town only became significant with the arrival of a rail link from the nearby town of Kanash in 1939. It has a mixed Chuvash and Russian population.

At about 9am we disembarked and were loaded onto coaches, counted and the coach door closed ready for another tour of another city. As the coach driver Stanislav manoeuvred us around the streets the local tour guide Tamara pointed out the highlights of the city such as the largest dental surgery in the city and the first chemist to be established. We stopped and were directed into an entertainment hall where a 'tacky' costumed music group sang to us, giving an artificial recital of Chuvash folk songs such as would never exist in real life. That over we climbed back onto the coaches and visited the Holy Trinity Orthodox Monastery in the old town area, where head scarves were again handed out for the ladies to wear, as well as a visit to the classical columned House of Culture. Overall, it was a pleasant city with good open spaces. As we were taken on a walkabout overlooking one of these spaces Tamara, who must have been between forty and fifty years old, told the moving story of how she was baptised as an adult only in 1995 after the fall of communism. Her mother had had Tamara's brother baptised as an infant at the time of the communist regime and had then been called in by the communist authorities and threatened not to do that again and came very close to being sacked from her teaching job as a result. Therefore, she had deferred Tamara's baptism.

We had the obligatory visit to the war memorial, approached through a display of military equipment including tanks, aeroplanes and helicopters with a typical Soviet statue on a mound, an eternal flame and a construction of crumbling thin red granite. Only on closer inspection did I realise that this was in the shape of Afghanistan and the long list of names above was of the young men whose lives were wastefully and tragically thrown away in that Soviet campaign. A few locals were there at the memorial, remembering their loss.

Back on the coach, counted again and returned to the boat we had lunch as the crew sailed us the two and a half hours on to Kosmodemyansk, the second largest city in the Mari El Republic of Russia. This settlement, on the south bank of the Volga at the junction of that river with the Vetluga river, was founded in 1583 as a frontier fortress and named after Saints Cosmas and Damian and served as a way stop for travellers heading east. It became a city in 1781.

Safely moored at the river port our tour guide on the old and battered bus was Gennady who gave a commentary as we went around the quiet and sleepy city, surrounded by stillness and where even the birds were silent. We halted and got off to wander around an exhibition of old buildings including a windmill, then drove on to have a look at the solidly built and brightly painted brick Cathedral of the Theotokos of Smolensk with the usual onion domes and a separate bell tower. We then returned to the boat, walking through an avenue of souvenir stalls selling cheap nick knacks but where I was able to buy some decent fridge magnets to take home for the family.

Now all back on the boat again it left the river bank and headed into the river's flow. During dinner one of the regular waiters was missing and we learned that he had become too home sick and had been given permission to leave and head back to his family in Rostov-on-Don. That was a great shame but it did make us appreciate the difficulties of being a crew member on a cruise boat, working long hard hours to serve holiday makers and keep them happy, making the trip pleasant for them, and probably for not much pay. Apart from those we saw such as the waiters, bar staff and group leaders, entertainers, language teachers and reception staff and, I believe somewhere on board, hairdressers, there were also those hidden away from public view such as cooks, kitchen staff, cleaners, administrators, engineers and other crew doing a whole variety of tasks. Their accommodation and facilities would not be as good as ours. Our trip north would take two weeks. If all of the staff spent another two weeks on the return trip they could be away from home for a month, which could be a strain.

The scheduled after dinner entertainment was entitled 'Mister Cruise Show'. Really? No thanks, that was definitely not for me. I took my book outside and read.

That night sleep came only fitfully and all sorts of worries, fears and anxieties went round in my head. I decided it was better to get up and have a walk outside than to stay unsettled and struggling but it was a bit eerie going around dark, empty decks. I definitely decided that it would be a bad idea to fall overboard with absolutely no-one around to see me go and so watched my step carefully. Nevertheless, I stayed in the fresh air for a little while, following the marker buoys showing the boat the route to take until these mysteriously disappeared. Eventually I returned to my cabin and was able to doze off.

OLD, OLD RUSSIA

WEDNESDAY WAS A WARM day with clear skies. This was the ninth of May, Victory Day, a day of remembrance, parades and celebration of the triumph of the Soviet Union over Nazi Germany. I had an early breakfast with Roy and Edna during which Roy shared that he used to be an industrial chemist before they both took over the running of a nautical approved school before retiring. What a change of career!

We docked at Nizhny Novgorod, with its kremlin guarding the river, before seven o'clock in the morning. Nizhny Novgorod was founded in 1221 by the prince of Vladimir and is situated at the meeting of the Volga with the Oka river. Its raison d'etre has always been as a major trading centre. In Soviet times it was renamed, in 1932, to Gorky after the writer Maxim Gorky, a hero of the communist establishment, and was a closed city with no foreigners allowed. It returned to its original name in 1991.

Once moored and key handed in and down the gangway I expected us to be put straight onto the coaches waiting on the quayside. However, on this occasion things were different. We were assembled and then taken on foot across the shore road for a look around the nearby beautiful Stroganov church, or more accurately the Church of the Nativity of the Blessed Virgin Mary, built in the seventeenth century by the merchant Grigory Stroganov. It was very impressive with its brightly coloured domes. I was able to climb the hill behind the church to get a better view and was surprised to find a Spar grocers, previously common in the United Kingdom, on the road at the top!

It was only then, to keep to routine, that we walked back to the shore road and were loaded up onto the coaches and counted. Our coach driver was introduced as Oleg by the city guide who would commentate for us. He was called Anton.

As we drove around the city the guide explained that only two cruise boats were allowed at the river port at any one time, which today was our Anton Chekhov and a boat called the Igor Stravinsky. Anton described various things we could not see, such as a magnificent city hall hidden away behind trees. This caused an American in our group to moan 'first they get us up early, then they tell us we're not going to see anything'. I couldn't disagree. However, we did get off the coach to see the typical small Soviet flat in a low rise block which used to be the residence of Maxim Gorky and has now been turned into a museum. I decided that this museum was not for me and with Katya's permission I went and wandered the streets which were full of similar residential blocks, being careful not to get lost, and eventually, being near the shore road, I saw some of that day's military parade of armoured vehicles and tanks forming up. I got back in time to be driven on the coach to the pedestrianised city centre.

There were big crowds forming in this pedestrianised area, undeterred by a sudden heavy rain shower. Metal detector gates were set up at the end of the street and around the square in front of the high walled kremlin and these were guarded by soldiers with fierce looking dogs. This was where the main parade would be held. As we left the coach Katya warned us not to go through the gates into the square because the crowds would stop us getting out again. Nevertheless, we watched the Parade of Veterans - grey haired survivors of the Second World War - line up on the unrestricted side of the gates in smart suites and military uniforms bedecked with medals and with tulips in their hands and we saw them march off with a band towards the centre of events. As well as us seeing them off they were also seen off by cadets dressed in caps and white shirts and ties, holding high mainly black and white photos of past soldiers in readiness for the March of Heroes.

Crowds were building up significantly, all heading towards the kremlin area, so after a little while Katya called us together to go against the flow of people back to the coach parked a short distance away. We all returned safely to the boat. However, we found out later that that was not the case for everyone. One of the German passengers, so not on Katya's coach, did go into the main square and was left behind. Katya explained what I had already heard, that that gave them a real problem since the staff have to get money from the boat's purser and also stay behind until the errant passenger is found. Then they have to get a taxi to catch up with the boat. However, the overstay of this person ended well. Apparently, after our boat had set sail the passenger concerned was taken onto another boat and transferred mid-river without our captain having to dock again.

The parade was still not underway as I sat on deck and watched the towers of Nizhny Novgorod's kremlin disappear into the distance. After lunch there was a presentation of Russian costumes given by the boat's shop staff of which I kept well clear. A little later in the afternoon there was another Russian language class led by Katya. That I thought I would attend and, having sat in the back of the Russian language class for the German passengers with no sign of Katya and not understanding either language, I eventually found the correct Russian for English speakers' class in another room and slipped in unnoticed. Neither class improved my language skills one jot.

The time of the Russian songs class in the late afternoon found me on deck where I watched with fascination as the boat skilfully negotiated with precision positioning another couple of locks at another dam, this time in the company of the cruise boat Borodino, with both boats accompanied by flocks of birds looking for tasty scraps. However, I did go to the 'Romantic Russia' concert including some dancing given by the boat's musicians supported by other tour staff and crew which was very enjoyable and a break from my normal routine.

The further north we travelled the more varied became the weather and after dinner there was heavy rain, thunder and lightning. Sitting on the sheltered rear deck watching the storm I was joined by a pleasant Dutch couple who revealed that they had travelled all over the world including Tibet. I had no resentment, jealousy or feeling of inferiority at all hearing that but I did realise what a novice I was.

Thursday started really early, well before full light, with breakfast from 6.30 to 8am. I joined a couple of Germans in the dining room who were very friendly but whose English was limited. However, I did understand them to say that they too, similar to my breakfast companions a few days ago, had been on the Anton Chekhov last year cruising from Moscow to St Petersburg but with a completely different tour and restaurant staff. Another German joined us, from northern Germany, and who had been to Russia seven times. He was using the cruise to learn French and walked around the decks with cards trying to absorb vocabulary but I had not noticed him yet so maybe he kept his pacing to the upper deck. Today it was overcast and drizzling and so he would find something else to do.

Breakfast finished I said 'excuse me' to my eating companions and went out under the sheltered deck to see what was happening. We were due into Kostroma but were idling in mid-stream for ages while we waited for the Igor Stravinsky cruise boat to dock. The clouds and the drizzle meant that even now it was still half-light outside. Nevertheless, eventually we were tied up alongside the Igor Stravinsky and just after 8am we walked through that boat to the coaches on the river bank to be counted and taken for our viewing of Kostroma.

Kostroma was founded in 1152 where the Kostroma river meets the Volga and developed as a market town. In the eighteenth century it was given a classical street pattern of radiating streets with squares and columned trading arcades. Its kremlin was destroyed in the Russian civil war.

On the other side of the Kostroma river from the city we visited the white walled Ipatiev monastery with its green conical hats to the towers, its magnificent green and yellow entrance gate decorated with friezes and its golden onion domed churches inside and where, in 1613, a delegation of citizens insisted that the eighteen year old Mikhail Romanov accept the Russian throne. As we had approached the monastery I had noticed a large abandoned timber built church nearby with five onion domes atop a pitched roof and fenced around but sneaked off anyway to have a little look at that. However, I made sure I returned in time to be counted back onto the coach. We were next dropped off in the town centre to have a look at the trading arcades with their classical columns, an old yellow painted fire watch tower and the nearby statue of Lenin described as 'the most ridiculous statue in Russia'. Looking at it one could not tell whether it was intended to be that way or had just come out of the cast badly but certainly it was unusual and I wouldn't be surprised if the sculptor had ended up in the Gulag for his efforts.

We eventually returned to the boat, chatting among ourselves as we went. During lunch Katya came to the table and whispered for Peter and me to be in reception at twelve noon the next day for something special but to keep it strictly to ourselves. How mysterious and 'cloak and dagger'!

The next stop, in the middle of the afternoon, was Yaroslavl, situated at the confluence of the Volga and Kotorosl rivers and founded by the Kievan Prince Yaroslavl in the eleventh century to secure his principality's north-eastern flank. For a time in the early middle ages it was one of the most important cities in the land. Now it is an industrial centre with a population of approximately six hundred thousand people.

As we approached the river port, welcomed in by the golden onion domes of a cathedral overlooking the river, I could see that two cruise boats, the Igor Stravinsky and the Lenin, were already docked. We moored alongside and walked through both to get to the waiting coach manned by the local tour guide Olga, a full time guide and a native of the city. Olga explained that not many foreign tourists cruise the Volga and her work is primarily to guide Russian visitors although Russians tend not to visit that far from Moscow and find it cheaper to go abroad than travel within Russia. She commented that the seasonal temperature differences are less in Yaroslavl than elsewhere since in winter it only drops to around minus ten degrees Celsius and being a 'dry' cold the population do not even need to wear face masks. I think I would!

We were taken to the Monastery of the Transfiguration of the Saviour founded in the twelfth century and enclosing a sixteenth century cathedral within its walls and at that time one of the most prominent and prosperous monasteries in the lands of Muscovy. There I was able to grab a coffee and another large bottle of water and watch the black robed and anorak-clad priests ringing the small bell ensemble in the grounds. We moved on to the Church of Elijah the Prophet built by fur traders in the seventeenth century and located in the centre of the city, opposite the town hall, and painted white with bright green onion domes, and then to the Annunciation Cathedral which had been our first sight of the city as we approached on the river and is on a spit of land overlooking the Volga. This is a new cathedral with titanium covered domes since the previous historic building was demolished by the communists. Not all churches in the city were treated that way, with some being turned into museums or concert halls. Inside a railinged enclosure next to this cathedral was an ensemble of large bells. The priests rang these by standing inside them and swinging the clappers, which apparently was less noisy for them, and therefore better for their ears. There was a very well kept and moving war memorial on the same site as this cathedral with wreaths and flowers at its foot.

While we were being bussed around Yaroslavl the boat left the river port to be refuelled but was there to take us back on board when the city tour was finished.

Dinner was a bit later that evening and served while we were still docked. Departure was between the main course and dessert and both Peter and I again left poor Rosemary so we could watch this. As we chugged along the river for our next planned stop at Uglich the following morning I sat in my now usual place and successfully avoided that evening's entertainment, the last part of the film 'Russia - the Land of the Czars Part IV'. I was glad I did for a few miles after Yaroslavl we passed, at a distance away, a couple of redundant churches without their domes, just the tower stalks, and they looked very forlorn. A few times during the trip I had wanted to take a photograph but felt that the camera I had lacked a decent zoom. This was one of those times and I made a note to look into getting a better quality device for my next trip. My next trip? What was I thinking! I had read that the impressive Tolga Convent, dating from the seventeenth century, was on this part of the river. I moved and sat on the port side where I was expecting this to be but I was beginning to think that I'd missed it. For no particular reason I decided to stretch my legs and as I strolled along the other side of the boat there it was, all domes and bright pristine paintwork. I was so pleased that I hadn't missed it but so cross with myself for getting the wrong bank.

Overnight, as I slept, the boat went through another lock and entered the Rybink Reservoir from where it turned into the final length of the Volga heading south-west. I was sorry that I missed this reservoir stage of the journey but at some point I did have to sleep!

The end of the cruise was approaching and as I got up on the Friday morning I realised that there was now only one more stop before Moscow. The cruise had gone quickly, I had had a few days of real relaxation away from the stresses that faced me at work but the real world was now fast approaching. Nevertheless, I had two days left and so I pushed those thoughts to the back of my mind.

I shared breakfast with a lovely couple, a Dutch husband and his English wife who lived in Holland and were part of a Dutch group on the boat that I had failed so far to identify. She had first visited Russia as a student in the 1960s, revisited in 1993 with her husband and returned now, noticing the changes that had occurred on each revisit.

After breakfast I went outside and watched as Uglich, with its large dam and hydro-electric station and with the Lenin and Igor Stravinsky boats already moored, came into view. As the town got closer I noted a fire watch tower, probably eighteenth or nineteenth century, near the river port, about a hundred yards away from it. There was room for us to moor to the quay rather than to the other boats and I thought that if I was one of the first off the boat I would have plenty of time to wander over and have a look at this tower, before joining my group for what was to be a walking tour.

As the crew started dealing with the mooring ropes a crowd assembled in the reception area. I had already handed in my key so sneaked through the outside door to be behind the edge rails but well away from the crew activity and better placed for a quick exit once the gang plank was in place. Unfortunately, as I quietly waited, one of the other passengers made an exclamation in a language I didn't understand and a crew member beckoned me inside and showed me the notice saying I shouldn't have been standing where I was whilst mooring was going on. I'd been 'snitched' on. Slightly awkwardly and in front of all the other passengers I had to go to the back of the crowd. The best laid plans can go wrong! Once disembarked I did rush over to the fire watch tower and back to the group but it wasn't the leisurely stroll I had intended.

Uglich is notorious as the place where the son of Ivan the Terrible, Dmitry, met his death in 1591. This was thought to have been on the orders of Boris Godunov, his foster father, who then became Czar, although this has never been proved. Dmitry's death heralded the start of the Time of Troubles which only ended when Mikhail Romanov was offered the throne in 1613.

Our group number five had the local tour guide Luba who walked us to the nearby kremlin area with its fifteenth century Prince's Chambers House, the 1690s Church of St Dmitry on the Blood and the petite Transfiguration Cathedral built on the site of a previous church in 1713. We were told the story of the old church bell which was flogged, had its tongue - its clapper - pulled out and for many years was banished to Siberia and as we were shown the churches with their wall and ceiling paintings Luba explained the ornate sanctuary screens that separate the nave, the peoples' area, from the chancel, the priests' area, and which extend from floor to ceiling with doors in the centre. The screens have rows of painted figures and icons and apparently the most important picture is on the lowest level and is the second to the right of the doors. Usually this is a representation of the person after whom the church is named. The church domes at roof level outside have Christ represented by the central dome with the four evangelists, Matthew, Mark, Luke and John represented by the corner domes and with colours also being of significance - green for the Spirit, blue for the Virgin and gold for hospitality.

Being a walking tour we had freedom to wander around the area and relax. I managed to buy some more souvenir fridge magnets at a kiosk and again some water. However, eventually we were herded together and returned to the boat.

Immediately after leaving the river port we negotiated a lock at the town's dam and then it was time to join Katya in the reception area to see what all the mystery was about. I was very intrigued.

Those of us nominated by Katya, six of us, duly and discreetly assembled and were led by Katya and her colleague Anna through a small door into the staff quarters, past kitchens, laundries and stores until we came, at last, to the purpose of the exercise - the engine room! This was the inner sanctum of the boat and not even Katya and Anna had been there before, let alone any passengers. We were so privileged. The size of the yellow painted engines was huge and the smell of oil and grease intoxicating. The area was manned and kept very clean by four engineers. Sensibly we were kept to the entry gantry and not allowed to wander as the Chief Engineer ran through some mechanical facts and figures.

Questions were invited and I asked how the engines would be removed if that became necessary. I was told that the dining room and decking above was removable but that the boat itself was more likely to need replacing before the engines. Then I mentioned how one night the boat had followed lit buoys until these disappeared and the Chief Engineer said that the boat would have been guided by radar. Finally, I asked whether the engineers ever saw daylight which brought a smile to their faces and the answer 'occasionally'. All in all it was a very satisfactory visit and well worth missing the first part of lunch to complete it.

When Peter and I did arrive at our lunch table we had another passenger sharing the meal. We introduced ourselves to Hank, an American in his late seventies. The others on his usual table had been two elderly New Zealand ladies but they had transferred to another boat so rather than sit on his own he had accepted Rosemary's invitation to join us and he was good company. He was a widower and after his wife's death had taken to travelling the world and he told us tales of his adventures.

Lunch finished and out in the fresh air I forsook a Question and Answer session on the Russian Way of Life Today and instead put together a note to thank the room cleaner for keeping my cabin spotless and tidy. I only saw her a couple of times but really appreciated her efforts. Having drafted the note I took it to the reception staff who kindly undertook to type a translation for me.

As the afternoon went on Katya gathered her group together and explained that the last sailing evening of the cruise, this evening, was a time when a talent show was held, with each group performing an item. I had noticed 'Talent Show' on the day's itinerary but had not reckoned on participating! However, all in the group who were able were expected to join in. This was something that was obviously a regular feature of the cruise and Katya had a version of 'Cinderella' all ready and handed out scripts for the various roles. My role was being part of a crowd and I was very happy to be confined to that.

Then the Australian man, Neville, who had the role of Prince Charming, said 'Oh, Landers would be far better' and backed away, leaving me in prime spot. Thank you very much Neville. Nevertheless, after taking a few deep breaths I decided to run with it. We had a couple of rehearsals and felt as prepared for the evening performance as we ever would be. The day was not going as I had intended!

THE END

IT WAS LATER ON in Friday afternoon that I became aware of the boat's engines slowing from their steady throb and then idling and the boat drifting. I looked around from my usual spot on deck and finally noticed why. The captain was giving passengers the opportunity to view an isolated baroque style bell tower on a small islet emerging from the water, all that remained of a larger church building that had existed before a reservoir was formed. It was a sad yet somehow impressive monument which spoke to the history of the river and its settlements and the sacrifices made for the sake of 'progress'.

I returned to my cabin after that and expected to find the translation of my note to the cleaner but nothing was there so I wandered up to reception to enquire. They said they had left a finished copy on my cabin door handle but there was no sign of anything so they kindly did it again. Then, instead of spending time at the captain's farewell drinks in the bar, although I could have attended if I'd wanted, I sat on deck with my phrase book and English-Russian dictionary checking that the reception girls had not slipped any naughty words into their final typed message! They hadn't although some of the phraseology was different but with the same meaning. I copied the short note onto a spare postcard to leave for the cleaner on the last day. That day was fast approaching and the dread of returning to work came with it but there was the challenge of the talent show to distract me from such thoughts.

After the evening meal, which again had Hank joining us, the passengers assembled for the show. Those of us in Group 5 joined the audience to watch the other acts. Some acts were singing, some were reciting poetry and then it was our turn. We took our places on the stage with me sitting near the centre. Katya put my prop, a shoe, Cinderella's shoe, under my chair in readiness. We started and I followed the script carefully. As my lines approached

I felt under the chair for the shoe. No shoe. I felt again. No shoe, I couldn't find it. Then it was too late to search anymore so employing my best theatrical improvisation I mimed and pretended that I was holding a shoe, made sure people realised that by smelling the imaginary footwear, and I got away with it. The production went well, polite applause followed and afterwards the missing shoe was returned to Katya from well behind my chair where it was definitely out of reach.

Although there had been only the one stop, at Uglich, the day had been really busy and after watching the crew take us through yet another series of locks and having a final bed time coffee and a quiet ukulele strum I settled down contentedly tired and slept soundly.

Saturday was to be a relaxed day. In the early hours a couple of locks were negotiated but I had no awareness of that. We had then entered the last length of the Volga, now heading south rather than north, and with a noticeable increase in the number of bulk carriers sailing by, before the boat went through two locks with towers at each end and finally started its journey down the Moscow Canal, eighty kilometers long and built between 1933 and 1937 by two hundred thousand Gulag prisoners and also flowing through some lakes, so giving Moscow access to the Volga river system. The traversing of this canal would take a very long time at very low speed.

I read through breakfast and then observed from outside the many abandoned industrial sites, disused dock cranes and various ships and boats in various states of repair, including mere shells, that lined the way. A film of our particular cruise was shown in the lounge throughout the morning on a continuous loop but I decided that I could do without that entertainment. The boat's shop held a tombola which I also decided I could do without.

This was the morning for the settling of bar bills. It had been announced the day before and I had tried to settle mine that evening but been told to wait. So wait I did and in the middle of the morning joined a queue in the bar and settled my bill in cash for just one drink of lemonade taken on the first day of the cruise. I paid in roubles but got given a Euro coin as change which I didn't think was quite right and insisted on roubles which came as notes. I would be able to exchange those when I got home. I was very relieved that I had avoided using the bar and having a drink at meals since it would have been easy for the bill to run away and other passengers were settling fairly high amounts.

We were definitely not entering the smart end of Moscow but it was nevertheless interesting. During lunch Katya checked who was signing up for the optional tours of 'Moscow by Night' and for the Metro tour that evening and also for the Tretyakov Gallery and the Circus show tomorrow. I opted out of all of those.

It was some time after lunch that we arrived in Moscow River Port basin, which was crowded with at least fifteen other cruise boats present. We moored alongside the Rachmaninov. The by now familiar routine of getting onto coaches was followed again in the early afternoon and we were driven into central Moscow. The guide, Tatiana, explained the horrendous traffic that regularly grid locked the city centre but we seemed to avoid this as we were taken to the fashionable Arbat shopping street, which did not seem to have any special shops, nor be all that busy and which I found disappointing. Maybe it was because it was towards the end of the afternoon. Then it was off to a lovely park and lake behind which was the seventeenth century Novodevichy Convent, now a UNESCO World Heritage Site. This convent is the place where the communist high and mighty are buried. When I realised that we were not going up to the convent but only viewing this from the far side of the park I checked with Katya and she gave me five minutes to run across the park, around the lake and get a decent nearer look. Five minutes was enough. Next we were taken by coach to the Cathedral of Christ the Saviour with our guide telling us that the original was blown up by the communists in the 1930s and the new cathedral was built from 1995, with the rebuilding taking five years to complete. At a nearby kiosk I was able to grab an ice cream and again a bottle of water. Then it was on to the university, one of Stalin's Seven Sisters skyscrapers which was on a height from where we were able to enjoy good views across the city. Finally, it was onto Red Square with its Lenin Mausoleum and the GUM store with its atrium and glazed roof and upmarket stores.

As we were taken back to the boat there were whispered discussions among the passengers about how much to tip the staff. In my naivety I had never even considered the idea of tipping and now realised that I was moving among a different social class. I was on a budget and could not afford for tips to break that. Helpfully the boat circulated guidelines for tipping saying that these could be general or marked for any specific crew member and fortunately I had an envelope so no one would know how much I donated. I decided that I wouldn't be influenced by the other passengers, who would be likely to have more funds than me, but I would give what I could. When the time came and the tip box was set up later in reception I split my tip, half for the general fund and half for Katya, and I set the total at a proportion of the roubles I had left. Whilst I would not need roubles once home I kept some back to cover any emergencies over the next day or so.

Returned to the boat and with a little time before dinner I avoided the inevitable scramble at reception to collect cabin keys and instead of heading on board I walked along the quayside to look at the fenced off, but with see-through wire fencing, derelict two storey river port building. This was of constructionist design and made to look like a boat. Interesting painted roundels were present on the columns showing various Volga river scenes. I then strolled into the nearby residential areas, using the dilapidated underpass to cross the busy dual carriageway road separating these from the port, and found the River Port metro station. That would be for what I was planning for the last full day, Sunday, tomorrow.

A good dinner that evening was again shared with Hank and I was able to inspire Peter to also go and explore the river port building. Meanwhile after dinner a number of passengers went off for the Moscow by Night and Metro tours and I sat outside reading, writing, looking at the exhibition submarine and sea planes on the other side of the river basin and again thinking of my return to work.

Going to sleep that night was more difficult and I missed the gentle rocking movement of the boat in motion.

I woke up on Sunday, as I have said the last full day, with my return to work still on my mind. However, a good breakfast, shared again with John and Wendy talking about their Nile cruises, pushed these thoughts out of my head. Our itinerary for the day instructed those who were going on the Kremlin tour to collect a packed lunch before leaving the dining room, which I duly did. Keeping a close track of time I nipped back to my cabin and put out my thank you card for the cleaner where she could see it and then at nine o'clock we were counted onto the coaches and taken into the centre of the city to the Kremlin where the same guide as yesterday would show us around. Thankfully, as a tour party, we didn't have to queue to get in.

The Kremlin was familiar to me now after last year's visit and we were taken to the same areas but I was very pleased to be seeing it all again. I was able to focus on different things and what struck me particularly this time were the extensive grounds and tulip beds. The guide explained more about Orthodox worship which was interesting. Apparently services can last two to three hours and at certain parts of the service everyone has to stand still but other parts are flexible and allow walking around and even leaving and returning. The sanctuary screens have five rows, from top to bottom showing prophets, apostles, festivals, Christ with the angels and his disciples and finally local saints. Wall paintings in churches tell Bible stories, especially the Fall of Man. Icons show a saint and scenes from his life and his 'miracles'. With respect to bells, the deeper the tone the better is the connection with Heaven. Whenever a Czar was crowned a new bell was cast. As with last year we did not go to the Armoury with its Faberge collection. Still, not seeing those would justify a third visit at some point!

After the Kremlin the coaches were ready to take us back to the boat but I was keen, and had laid my plans, to do some exploring on my own. Checking again with Katya and with map in hand and with my phrase book telling me how to ask for a single ticket on the Metro to get me to the River Port Station and leaving from which platform, I was given my freedom but again with strict instructions from Katya not to get lost.

I wanted to see Pushkin Square, often a place of dissent and protest. That was within an easy walk of the Kremlin so I headed north away from there and found it successfully, seeing the statue of Pushkin and the first McDonald's to ever open in Russia, which was on 31st January 1990. This was such an innovation that the queue at the opening was approximately thirty-eight thousand people and went many, many times around the block. I did note that the roads in that area of Moscow had some very static traffic jams. From there I went back past the classical Bolshoi Ballet building and on to the Lubyanka, a seven or so storey cream and ochre painted luxury hotel taken over in 1926 by the KGB as their headquarters, and from where I strolled into Red Square with its Lenin and Stalin lookalikes seeking photo opportunities from the many tourists. As I then walked along the Moskva river for a bit my nerve began to fail me. I was not actually that bold or daring finding my way around this city, albeit a lovely city, and so after a couple of hours I popped into a cafe for a coffee and a rest.

After that I made for a metro station, Teatralnaya, on the metro green line number two which would take me, without the need to change, to the River Port station. I bought a ticket for one journey from the lady in the ticket kiosk, went to the platform, let several trains come and go until I was happy I knew the direction I needed and then sat on a train until it got to my destination, carefully reading each station name and following progress on the metro map in the carriage. From there I knew my way back to the boat and on arrival reported back to Katya so she knew that I had not gone missing.

In terms of adventures it hardly registered but for me it was a big step forward, out and about on my own in a foreign city with no language skills and reading Cyrillic text, and my confidence jumped upwards. I felt that I could actually find my way around if I ever had to.

That night we missed Hank at our evening meal. He had opted out of the Kremlin tour and instead walked his wheeled suitcases up the quay to another boat on which he was going to travel up to St. Petersburg, then change again to cruise to Stockholm, then take a train to Hamburg from where he intended to hire a car and drive around Germany. I felt tired just hearing his plans but full of admiration.

I said goodbye to Peter and Rosemary who would be leaving early the next day. They had been excellent travelling companions.

It was now a much quieter boat as passengers dispersed and some of the groups left for home, wherever that may be. Katya came to our table and explained to Peter, Rosemary and me that we would need to be out of our cabins by ten o'clock tomorrow morning and then there would be only one passenger toilet available on the boat in the cabin nearest reception as a full deep clean of everywhere started ready for a quick turnaround and the next set of passengers.

Later, as it got dark, I packed up my cabin ready for my departure and return home and all that awaited me at work. In particular I made sure my camera cards were safe since the fourteen hundred photos they held were my record of a wonderful experience. I was pleased that after the rocky start to the trip I had settled into it, learned to mix with others and found the security of the boat and being looked after every step of the way reassuring. I would miss that as I headed back to reality. However, I was rested and refreshed and my head was now clearer. Generally, I had slept well, eaten well and had had plenty of distractions and social contact. Overall my mental health had strengthened and I was in a much better position to deal with whatever awaited me on my return to the office.

The final day, Monday, I woke up to a surprise. During the night the Rachmaninov and the Anton Chekhov had swapped places, maybe as part of a refuelling operation although that is my speculation, and I had neither heard nor felt anything. Up, showered and dressed I headed to the half empty dining room for a leisurely breakfast. My taxi wasn't due until 1.15pm and I had time to spare. I had a last conversation with John and Wendy and then a final check of my cabin before moving my luggage to the reception area. As I killed time I chatted with some others of the SAGA group who were waiting for their coach to appear and I had a final conversation with Roy and Edna. Eventually the SAGA group left, then others left and by mid-day it was just me remaining. I sat and read in the warm sunshine.

Katya kept an eye on me. She was staying on board to work her way to St. Petersburg and then flying home to Rostov-on-Don from there. This change over day was her busiest and the last thing she wanted was a stranded passenger. She checked my departure arrangements. 1.15pm came and no taxi but Katya was right on the case. I was going to give it another few minutes before getting worried - why I don't know given my previous experiences - but rightly Katya said 'No. Let's 'phone them now' and taking the JGR 'phone number from me made the call. After some exchange in Russian with the person on the other end of the 'phone she was reassured and within ten minutes a battered taxi appeared.

There was a great deal I wanted to say to Katya by way of thanking her for showing me her lovely country but in the end I could only manage a simple 'Thank you. Goodbye' as I headed down the gangway to the waiting driver, who stopped smoking as I got into the scruffy car with my luggage. As we went off I decided not to look back.

The driver turned onto the dual carriageway outside the river port and then spent an hour negotiating urban roads before we reached the busy Moscow ring road. This was taking much longer than I expected and as I checked my watch I began to get worried. After two hours we were still on the ring road and I was getting fearful of missing my flight home. It started to rain, beginning light and then getting heavier, which slowed the traffic. Finally, after almost three hours we pulled up outside of the glass fronted Domodedovo airport terminal building and I grabbed my bags and walked quickly inside with regret that I had not just jumped onto the metro and then taken an express train which I could have caught earlier and would have been quicker and less stressful.

There was a security check at the terminal entrance which I negotiated successfully and then I picked up my boarding card from the British Airways desk. Going through border control with my landing card returned I passed a second security check without problems and with my travel kettle element unchallenged and then got my bearings, checked the departure boards and sat down to get my breath back and wait a little while for the gate announcement. As I waited I was pleased to see several other passengers from the boat also waiting for their flights. It wasn't long before the departure gate was shown and I made my way there.

Smart and efficient hostesses checked my passport and boarding card at the head of the gantry and their colleagues welcomed me on board the plane. As is my habit I shut my eyes and gripped the arm rests during take-off and, after an uneventful four hour flight with an edible meal and a not particularly communicative person sitting next to me, I did the same on landing at Heathrow. As the aeroplane taxied a man stood up to get out of his seat before the seat belt signs were switched off and straight away a stewardess was down the aisle, hands onto his shoulders and pushing him back down. However, immediately on stopping people leapt up to grab hand luggage from the overhead lockers. I let the rush go and was happy to tag along at the back of the queue and then, with hand luggage only, went straight to border control, through the customs green channel and, after fishing out my preloaded Oyster card, onto the underground

Piccadilly Line into central London. A short walk from Leicester Square underground station took me to Charing Cross and a train to my home station. Having walked the few minutes from there to my house I rang the front door bell and walked in satisfied and happy at completing the trip and braced and ready for the forthcoming battle with my manager.

AN ADVENTURE TO THE GOLDEN RING

TRAVEL TO OLD RUSSIA

THE GOLDEN RING

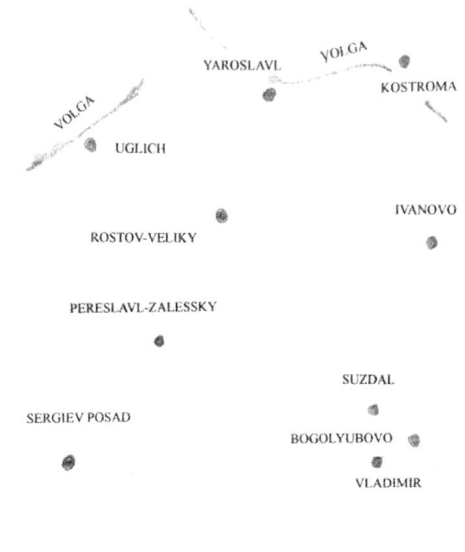

VOLGA

YAROSLAVL VOLGA

KOSTROMA

VOLGA

UGLICH

IVANOVO

ROSTOV-VELIKY

PERESLAVL-ZALESSKY

SUZDAL

SERGIEV POSAD

BOGOLYUBOVO

VLADIMIR

MOSCOW

DIY

IT WAS A WARM Saturday in the middle of September and I knew I wasn't being very good company.

Good friends had kindly invited my wife and me, together with four or five other couples, to a weekend house party with them at a home they owned near the centre of Ramsgate. We had been to similar house parties in other years and the usual Saturday afternoon activity was to walk along the sea front beneath the cliffs to nearby Broadstairs, have a coffee and an ice cream, and then walk back to Ramsgate across the headland, a distance of about two miles each way.

However, this day I was so tired that I decided I could do nothing other than stay behind, lounge in the small sheltered garden at the back of the house and enjoy the sun's rays whilst drifting in and out of sleep. I wondered whether I was ill with something but eventually decided that it wasn't that. Instead, I was suffering from nervous exhaustion and that shouldn't have surprised me. After all, apart from all the usual stresses of life and work, I had, more pertinently, just come back from an adventure, my third adventure, in Russia!

The urge to return to Russia had come upon me in 2013, a year before this moment. I felt that I had unfinished business there and that my explorations of that country were not yet complete. I had been west to east and south to north but I still had places not seen that were a 'must' to see. I hadn't been to St Petersburg and I hadn't completed the Golden Ring cities and towns and I hadn't done the BAM or, to give it its full name, the Baikal Amur Mainline. This is a railway situated in eastern Siberia, parallel to, but three to four hundred miles north of, the Trans-Siberian railway and runs through very isolated and inhospitable wildernesses. Doing this had been the subject of discussion between Howard, June and me when we journeyed along the Trans-Siberian.

For several weeks I mulled things over and wondered what I should do. I wondered whether the BAM would be good and went as far as obtaining the book 'The Siberian BAM Guide' by Athol Yates and Nicholas Zvegintzov and asked JGR for a price, flying through Moscow to Krasnoyarsk, then by train to the cities of Severobaikalsk, Tynda, Komsomolsk-na-Amur and Khabarovsk, flying from there back to Moscow and home. The price they gave was reasonable, in the same region as my previous two trips with them, but at that point in time too much for me, and the duration, fourteen days, too long and I would be going solo which on reflection I didn't want to do. So that would not be for now but I filed the quote away for future reference.

That left St Petersburg and the Golden Ring. After lots of mind changing - Should I do this? Could I do that? Were there other possibilities? - I eventually, almost on the toss of a coin, opted to further explore the Golden Ring, and in particular to get to Suzdal, which was the prize I wanted to see most. Discovering St Petersburg would just have to wait that little bit longer. Exploring the BAM would have to wait a lot longer.

As always, over a few quiet evenings, I started reading and researching and also went straight back to the JGR website to see what they offered. They still advertised a Golden Ring tour but also including other destinations with that, such as Moscow and St Petersburg. The tour looked good - not escorted but fully organised with hotels, taxis and guides arranged - but the price, although very reasonable, was just too much for me. Also at the back of my mind was a fear that I would be doing the tour on my own. There was no guarantee that I would be with others. That was very ironic in view of what I eventually did. Anyway, I decided I would have to think again.

I was despondent for a few days but then pulled myself together. I worked out what I could afford and went back to JGR asking whether a bespoke tour was possible based on a part of their listed programme. What I had in mind was to fly to Moscow and then go to Vladimir, to the palace and monastery of

Bogolyubovo, to Suzdal and to Sergiev Posad only, all places on the Golden Ring. They worked out a good price for me, less than their standard tour yet sadly still more than I could readily manage financially. I hesitated, not really knowing what to do.

And that was the moment when Clare had a long and serious conversation with me.

Clare was my work colleague - I was still in the same job, had the same issues with my manager but was actively looking to escape elsewhere and in the meantime fighting off a nervous breakdown. Clare sat at the desk opposite mine and in many ways she and I were similar. We both knew exactly how the office ran and the absurdities of that. We both liked the idea of travelling but Clare was considerably more experienced at that than me. In a less busy moment when the telephones had stopped ringing, we quietly chatted about our aspirations to see the world, the 'where' and the 'when' and then we found ourselves discussing the 'how'.

'What you do' Clare said 'is to book the flights and once that's done you go onto Booking.com and look for somewhere to stay and if, when you get there, you don't like it you look on Booking.com again and find somewhere different. It's easy'.

Easy? To me that way of doing things seemed far from easy and was certain to be full of stress and would give me the opposite of a relaxing holiday. It would push me so far outside my comfort zones that I wouldn't be able to manage it and would collapse. However, Clare was firm. 'What's the problem? I do it and have never had any particular issues and so you can do it too' she said and with that encouragement, or was it admonishment, I realised that maybe her approach did work and could actually open up a whole world of new horizons for me. Instead of going wherever a tour company wanted to send me, to see whatever they wanted me to see, for however long they wanted me to see it and at whatever cost they chose to charge me, I could instead go where I wanted, see what I wanted and set my own timetable and my own budget.

But I plucked up my courage and challenged Clare. 'Wasn't it all just too risky? What if something went wrong? Who would rescue me? If I got lost would I ever be found again?'. However, after a certain amount of eye rolling she was firm again in her reply. 'Where's the risk?' she said, waving a finger at me and repeating 'You can do this'. 'Really?' I thought but I wasn't brave enough to say that out loud.

Despite my misgivings I did want to go and needed to go because, as mentioned, it was there as unfinished business and it would be a distraction from the torment that was my working environment, an environment which would eventually lead, at the beginning of the next year, to the total collapse of my health. So, as ever, over the next little while I did some more homework. Various evenings and weekends were spent, this time looking not so much at where to go but the practicalities. Previously I had taken the easy, convenient option, although it didn't always seem so at the time, but I knew Clare's way would not be that. If I organised things myself the booking of flights would be easy enough but how would I deal with getting a visa, with moving around from A to B, with communicating when I could neither speak nor understand Russian, with no one to turn to for advice, no one watching my back, no one giving me my meals, no one to point me in the right direction or find me if I really did get lost?

All of that was a lot to absorb and I had a conundrum. There were places to go but would my nerves and anxiety levels give me permission to get there? I hesitated. I researched. I decided for. I decided against. I was enthusiastic and ready to take the leap. I was petrified and wanted to play it safe. I was adventurous and brave. I was cautious and cowardly. What could I do? What should I do?

What I actually did was to get a piece of paper and scribble down the places I eventually decided were within my reach, namely Moscow, Vladimir, Suzdal and Sergiev Posad, together with a list of tasks. Flights? I could book those myself online and that wouldn't be a problem. Tick. Travel insurance? I scanned what was available online and that should only take a few 'phone calls. Tick. Visa? I thought back to the process I had gone through with JGR and the corrections they had made to my forms and the need for a letter of invitation. That would be difficult and I would definitely need help with that. Cross. Accommodation? Booking.com. Tick. Meals? I would just need to allow a reasonable sum for eating out. Tick. Moving around within Russia? I would need a train to Vladimir and could book the tickets for that online and allow something for bus fares to Suzdal and other train and metro fares. So a tick for that as well. Oh and my wife's permission to go. 'Yes, go on then' she said, looking to the sky and with a resigned sigh. Good. Tick.

I worked out a rough budget and this was within the right region for me but with respect to practicalities I would need some help, especially with the visa and, as I soon found out, also with trains. Commuter trains served Sergiev Posad and I was sure I could deal with those myself on the day. However, for the train to Vladimir I needed to make sure that was prebooked. I looked at the Russian railways website, the Russian railway company being RZD, and got lost and out of my depth after the first page. Not unreasonably it was all in Russian.

Eventually I was able to report back to Clare with a satisfied look on my face, telling her that I had booked flights online with Easyjet from London Gatwick to Moscow Domodedovo and back and accommodation for Vladimir and Suzdal through Booking.com and travel insurance with Direct Line, declaring my health conditions. However, I did have to confess that I was using a company, JGR, to sort out the visa, for a hotel in Moscow and for some trains, all pre-paid. Clare smiled in the way one does to a child, in a way that said 'See. That wasn't so difficult was it?' If only she knew the mental angst I had gone through just to get that far. Nevertheless, the die was cast and I was off again.

Excitement began to replace fear. I sorted out my visa application in the same way as my two previous trips, again with alterations made by JGR, in this case completely different hotels to those I put down, presumably something to do with aligning with the letter of invitation. JGR e-mailed to confirm the booking of the familiar Katerina Hotel in Moscow and train tickets to and from Vladimir. I checked my vaccinations and they were all still valid. I topped up the credit on my pay-as-you-go 'phone. I acquired some roubles, this time from Marks and Spencers, and a travel cash card in sterling to allow me to easily retrieve any unused content from a cash machine once home. I booked a taxi to Gatwick. I started sorting out maps, photocopying relevant pages from the guide books in my possession, searching and finding my previous maps of Moscow and finding a really useful 3D schematic map of Suzdal showing the main sights. I found a plan of Domodedovo airport with the Aeroexpress train station from there to central Moscow marked and I was able to book tickets for that on the translated Aeroexpress website. I wrote down useful Russian phrases in my notebook and wrote out place names and hotel addresses in felt tip in big, clearly legible lettering. This was a suggestion from my friend Andy and was really useful as a way of communicating and I have done this on subsequent trips. I made up a folder of papers, place names and maps for each day and got a rough idea of buses from Vladimir to Suzdal. I reviewed the lessons I learned on my previous journeys and in particular I invested in a camera of much better quality, a Canon digital camera, with a good 16x zoom, powered by AA batteries so no risk of any rechargeable battery failing, but still able to fit into my gilet pocket. I still use this camera and it has been one of my best acquisitions.

Google earth is a wonderful invention. I was able to remotely walk the streets from Paveletskaya station, where the Aeroexpress train terminated in Moscow, to the door of the Katerina hotel. I was able to view the train and bus stations at Vladimir and where the hotel was in that city. I walked through Suzdal until I found my accommodation. I found the way from Sergiev Posad train station to the monastery there.

I was now all set to go, had bags packed, gilet, belt bag and drawstring bag filled, some pot noodles and biscuits tucked away, clothes reduced to a minimum but all to return with me this time, flights there and importantly back booked in online a couple of weeks beforehand, as can be done with Easyjet unlike some other airlines when booking in can only be done twenty-four or thirty-six hours in advance. Other booking information was printed out, the visa was in my passport, roubles were in my pocket and scattered throughout my person and luggage, and my ukulele was securely tied onto my bag.

My emotions swung from excited expectation, with the adrenaline pumping, to absolutely terrified, also with the adrenaline pumping. My other two journeys had been out of my comfort zone but at least with other people, organised by companies who knew what they were doing and with some form, or so I felt, of a safety net. What I was doing now was an enterprise on a completely different scale and it was a leap into the unknown for me alone, on my own. If things went wrong there was no-one to help me or take responsibility. What lessons would I learn? Would I enjoy learning them or would they be painful lessons? Was I brave or silly? Time would tell. However, I had done the homework. All I needed to do now was pass the test.

On Friday 5th September 2014 I woke up early. In fact it was at about 3am and I wondered whether it had been worth my while going to bed at all. Creeping quietly around the house trying to miss any creaking floor boards so as to leave the sleepers undisturbed, I did a final check on my luggage, which I had left the night before set out neatly in the hallway, checked my documents, especially my passport and boarding card, had a breakfast and then went back upstairs. I said goodbye to my wife who mumbled incoherently before opening her eyes and managing to get out of bed and to her feet to see me off. My prebooked taxi arrived and with the usual passport check completed by the driver I was on my way.

The roads were already busy but the journey was smooth. The driver, a pleasant South African, said he did several trips to Gatwick airport each day. We chatted together and in no time at all we were pulling into the drop off zone of Gatwick's North

Terminal. I paid the requested fare and went inside the terminal building. Even at this hour there were many people around. Some were stretched out on the floor, presumably having slept there all night, a few were wandering around a bit aimlessly and a man in pilot's uniform was busy on his mobile 'phone trying to find his aeroplane and his crew mates!

With my preprinted boarding card I was able to go straight through the barriers into the usual and now familiar routine of security - watch off, no coins left in pockets, electrics and liquids into a tray, gilet, belt bag, drawstring bag and fleece into another, hand luggage bag and ukulele into yet another, all onto the conveyor belt and as they rumbled through the scanner I went through the metal detector gate. Eventually, and unchallenged, all my trays reappeared and taking them to one side I redressed and luggage in hand went to check the departures board. This told me that my flight was being shared with another airline. I checked gate locations, looked at my watch, found that I still had well over an hour to spare before boarding would start and so got myself a coffee from Pret which I consumed with the pastries I had packed for another breakfast, whilst all the time watching other passengers rushing around the busy waiting areas. Having also bought a couple of bottles of water I sat and read until the gate for my 7am flight was indicated.

Gatwick is a large airport and even with travelators the gate announced was fifteen minutes away from the main waiting area. With a little bit of rushing I managed to make it with plenty of time to spare and was checked through the boarding desk and followed other passengers to the ramps heading down to ground level and the aeroplane. That was the moment I had a scare. A uniformed man was at the top of the ramp scrutinising hand luggage and making sure passengers only had one piece each. Any extra had to go in the hold or be crammed into the allowed bag. My hand luggage bag was completely full and had no spare room to accommodate the contents of my drawstring bag. What do I do? Any hesitation would be fatal and mark me out for closer scrutiny so there was only one thing I could do. I slung my drawstring bag onto my back and boldly walked down the ramp. I got away with it, I think because the man got distracted by another passenger as I went past him. However, travelling on hand luggage only was, and still is, getting more and more difficult.

The aeroplane doors were closed on time at exactly 7am. At the start of the runway the plane paused and then, as it rumbled forward, I shut my eyes and gripped the arm rests and then we were off and airborne. I was in a middle seat with a sleeping Russian lady on the aisle side and a silent man on the window side, who also went to sleep. I resigned myself to an unsociable journey, pulled out my book and read between catching what glimpses I could of the foggy countryside flitting by beneath. There was no airline food on the flight - after all, this was a budget airline - but I did buy a coffee when the trolley came round and every so often I disturbed the sleeping lady to stretch my legs up and down the aisle. I completed the necessary landing card.

Approximately four hours after take-off we had a smooth landing, again eyes shut, arm rests gripped, and I had arrived at a sunny Moscow Domodedovo airport, without a cloud in the sky. I had returned to Russia yet again.

After the usual scramble to get off the plane I turned my watch forward three hours and successfully went through border control - 'purpose of visit?' 'Tourism', passport stamped, entry gate opened - and walked through customs and was ejected into the busy arrivals' hall. I was ready for the taxi driver onslaught which confronted me and happily walked through it with a 'Nyet, nyet, nyet' as I looked around and orientated myself. I knew roughly which way I should be heading for the Aeroexpress train but didn't want to walk the length of the airport just to walk all the way back again. I decided on the right direction, found the platforms, went through the barrier using the bar code on my ticket and looked at the waiting red painted train powered from overhead cables. 'Heading where?' I thought. I checked with a nearby official, showing them the name 'Paveletskaya Voksal' in large letters. Having received a 'da' I stepped in, found a seat and after a little while the sliding doors closed and the train headed off through a very familiar countryside of birch forest.

Eventually, after about an hour, the Moscow suburbs appeared with an array of various run-down building forms, until the train finally arrived at the large Paveletskaya station, just to the south of the very centre of Moscow. Exiting from the busy station was straightforward and once outside I found and stood in a discreet corner and breathed in again the atmosphere of a busy Moscow. Yes, I was back!

With map in hand, trying not to look like a lost tourist, I worked out which way I needed to walk to find my hotel. The last time I had stayed at the Katerina I had been dropped off at the hotel entrance and collected again by a guide or taxi. Now I would be looking for it on my own. I headed past an old lady begging on her knees outside the train station and went towards the embankment of the Moskva river, crossing roads at pedestrian crossings with others to make sure I didn't get run over. Look left right left and not right left right. I found the necessary section of the river embankment, occupied by a couple of fishermen patiently waiting for a bite, but could I see the hotel? No. In the end I asked a passerby who politely pointed to the large and unmissable, except by me, sign at roof level on the building opposite. I felt stupid but relieved. With thanks given I crossed the road and entered the hotel reception.

I had established a routine for entering hotels, shops and other such premises from my previous travels whereby I would immediately announce myself as a linguistically ignorant English-only speaker with no Russian language skills, by boldly saying 'Good morning' or 'afternoon' or 'evening' depending on the time of day. I slipped into that routine now with a clearly audible 'Good afternoon' and, at the same time that the Russian man behind the counter responded in perfect English, I offered up my passport. That was photocopied and returned to me with a room key and directions to the lift. I found the room without difficulty, a fourth floor double room at the front of the building next to the staircase and with an ensuite shower. I closed the room door behind me and looked around at the coloured furnishings, checked the free mini bar - only bottles of water and some crisps - and read the breakfast times in the information folder. I looked out of the window at the onion domes, four blue and one gold, on the church in the Novospassky Monastery, all dominated by its baroque style bell tower. I had arrived. I could begin to relax.

A little while later, showered and freshened up after my journey, I checked the time, chained and padlocked my luggage to the bed out of sight of the door, caught the lift back downstairs, settled into one of the comfy chairs in the reception area from where I could see the hotel entrance and waited. I didn't wait for long. At almost exactly the agreed time, 5pm, June's familiar face came into the building.

AWAY FROM MOSCOW

AS JUNE WALKED IN to the hotel I could see that she hadn't changed a bit and was the same as when we had last been with each other three year's previously. After returning home from our excursion together to Vladivostok she had retrained as a TEFL teacher, teaching English as a foreign language, then left her job in Swindon, taught in the former Yugoslavia for a while and then got a job teaching English in Moscow! We had kept in touch and I decided that it would be a shame to visit Moscow and not get together with her. As an aside, since Howard and I both worked in central London, we also kept in touch and had the occasional sandwich together until he took redundancy and then started travelling the world full time and in earnest.

June and I chatted over drinks for a while as she humorously recounted some of her many escapades in Moscow. Here I will relate just one.

On the very first day of her new teaching job she got lost. She took the wrong bus and ended up at a supermarket instead of a school. Knowing she was lost and getting distressed she went inside the shop looking for an English speaker to point her in the right direction since she, as a teacher of English, could not speak Russian. However, on finding no one she could communicate with she completely panicked and had a tearful blubbering meltdown. That brought the attention of the supermarket staff, who, learning from her paperwork where she should be, acted as if this was a perfectly normal occurrence and put her in a taxi at no charge and she arrived, very relieved, in her classroom only twenty minutes late.

The way June told the story was very funny. The effect it had on me, needing to catch the right bus from Vladimir to Suzdal and back, was very sobering!

Drinks finished we wandered out into the bright sunshine and walked the short distance along the river bank to Zaryadye Park and then on to St Basil's Cathedral, Red Square and the Kremlin walls, continuing to chat and catch up as we went. The mission I had that evening was to find and scout out Kursky and Yaroslavsky train stations and work out what was what so that I would be prepared for catching trains from them over the next few days and not get over anxious.

June took me on the metro to the impressively designed and decorated Komsomolskaya metro station, with its nearby Stalin's Sister high rise building and situated next to Yaroslavsky, the station I would need to get to for trains to Sergiev Posad, with Kazansky station, from where our Tran-Siberian adventure started, opposite. Yaroslavsky station building appeared to be shops and offices with the actual working station being uncovered and situated behind this with a bright green fascia. The ticket office that I would need was obvious beneath this fascia with barriers alongside and the platforms beyond. Good. We went back onto the metro and travelled a couple of stops to Kurskaya metro station, marble finished and with fancy red stars on the ceilings, serving Kursky main line station. We walked onto the massive concourse of the main line station with its huge glazed frontage. I had an electronic ticket for the trains to and from Vladimir, departing from this station, so wouldn't need the ticket office. However, I would need the platforms and they were nowhere to be seen. After standing and working out the various columns on the information board we started searching for the trains, to no avail until we came across an obscure flight of steps heading downwards. Exploring these we finally found what we were looking for, the platforms, trains, a waiting room and even a large chapel. I knew that such chapels are common at airports but hadn't expected one at a train station. It was a relief to find my way around Kursky station and I would certainly have panicked the next day when confronted with the dilemma of no trains! Somewhere there must have been another entrance to these, I am sure very clearly signposted and obvious, but we never found it.

The evening's mission accomplished we found a pizza outlet

nearby and went Dutch on a meal which both of us felt was adequate rather than brilliant.

As we ate June shared more about her life in Moscow, about the flat she shared with others who were not as considerate as her, about her work colleagues, most of whom she described as being in their mid-twenties but acting younger, and about her pupils who seemed to be typical inattentive teenagers with a sprinkling of other pupils down to the age of about four. She told how she once fell in the winter ice and how other Muscovites immediately rushed to pick her up since any time lying on freezing ground in Russia is dangerous. She had been visited by a friend earlier in the year and her parents were originally intending to visit next week. However, her dad had been taken unwell and they had had to cancel so instead she was heading back to her family home in Swindon for a few days, courtesy of Easyjet, this coming Wednesday evening. At that point I paused the conversation and in my mind checked my itinerary. 'Hang on' I said. 'That means that we're going to be on the same flight!' and that genuinely cheered us both.

Meal finished June kindly took me back to the Katerina to make sure I got 'home' safely, even though it was still daylight. We arranged to meet again the next day, exchanged mobile numbers and then, using her teaching skills, she set me the challenge of negotiating the metro on my own to meet her at Park Kultury metro station, just on the north bank of the Moskva river, telling me, as Clare had done 'You can do this'. We parted and she headed off to get her metro train back to her flat in the north-west of the city.

It had been a long but successful day. All on my own I had made my way to Moscow without any real anxiety. That night, after a text conversation with home as well as sending an e-mail home from the reception desk, and after a read and a quiet ukulele strum, I slept well, ready for the challenges of the next day.

That day, Saturday, came quickly. I was up early, showered, dressed, secured my bag and went down to the large hotel restaurant for a full breakfast of cereal, yoghurt, eggs, cold meats, pastries, coffee and fruit juice, showing my room key to the supervisor to gain entry. A good breakfast will sustain me through the day with little need to eat properly until the evening. There were no allocated tables so I picked one at random and sat down. As I ate I carefully examined my metro map in readiness for June's challenge and put in my notebook the stations through which I would pass, although actually there were only three. A full breakfast finished I gathered my possessions from the bedroom and booked out of the hotel, leaving my luggage in the security of the reception store room. Then, suffering from nervous fear, I headed to the metro, also at Paveletskaya, bought a ten token pass, easily done by holding up the relevant number of fingers at the ticket office window, and presented it to the barrier which stayed open as I walked through. If I hadn't tapped my pass the barrier would have shut on me as I went through. The escalator was very long, with the well-lit platforms thirty-three meters below ground level. Against the rules the occasional person sat on the escalator steps for the journey down. Once at the bottom I paused and spent a few minutes working out in which direction I needed to go by studying the route map posted high up on the wall. Finally I sorted that out, boarded a train and counted the stops. At the third stop I stepped out onto the platform, checked the name sign against what June had told me, rode up the escalator and, since there are no exit barriers on the metro, went straight outside to the fresh air. I was very pleased with myself for managing the metro on my own, a reminder of my previous effort a couple of years ago.

I was a little early, which was fine, so I was able to stand in a corner and watch the traffic and pedestrians rush by and take in the elegant exterior of the station with its reliefs of workers and all the time keeping an eye out for June coming from the exit. To my great relief she arrived about ten minutes later saying 'I knew you could do it'.

We started walking and crossed the river back to the south

bank. This time in Moscow I wanted to see things that I hadn't seen before but nevertheless we strolled into Gorky Park for a time before going to the fascinating Park of Arts on the opposite side of the road. This is absolutely full of displaced Soviet statues and sculptures, now out of keeping in the new post-communist Russia, and also with an artwork comprising a wall of carved stone heads behind mesh screens representing those imprisoned in the Gulags and which was quite moving. Unusually there was a very rare bust of Stalin, rare since nearly all representations of Stalin were destroyed after the fall of his reputation. We avoided the tractors with hose arrangements washing down the footpaths - lorries do the same to the roads - and admired the red squirrels. June explained that public spaces and parks such as Gorky Park and here were numerous and well-kept and respected since much of the population lived in flats without any private gardens.

Moving on from there we saw the Church of Christ the Saviour on the opposite river bank with its golden hemispherical domes and its lower areas surrounded by sheeted scaffolding and went past the modern ninety eight meter high Peter the Great statue, an ironic statue since Peter the Great loathed Moscow and this statue is similarly loathed by many Muscovites. We popped into a café for a drink and a snack and then took the metro together back to the hotel. My baggage now retrieved, June came with me to Kursky station where I now knew how to find the platforms. We arranged to meet next Wednesday evening to catch the plane and once my train to Vladimir was announced on the departure boards we went our separate ways, with June heading off to continue her weekend and me heading down the flights of stairs to the trains. I appreciated seeing June, realising after my just one night stay in the Katerina how isolating hotels can be, with no social contact. However, now I was alone.

I stood on the right number platform at Kursky station, as advertised on the information board, and was confused. This was a terminal station and I was expecting a train to be waiting but it wasn't. Instead, at the far end of the main platform was a raised section where a very smart, modern, red painted electric high speed train was standing. I had some time to spare so wasn't worried as I tried to work out what was going on. Passengers were boarding the high speed train and so I checked with someone who pointed me to that. I believe that the platform was split to accommodate the different boarding height between the older trains with their drop down steps and the newer trains with single step access. I counted down the number of carriages until I found my one, carriage No 2 at the far end, and joined a queue in front of a smartly uniformed attendant, with my electronic ticket and passport ready. When my turn came it was a quick check of my documents, a scan of my ticket and then I was motioned inside. I found my very comfortable allocated single seat by a window and settled into it and relaxed.

The train left on time and I listened carefully to the route announcement in Russian, the essential bits of which I understood - I was so proud of myself for that - and then heard the same announcement given in English. I thought that very useful but also a shame. However, I believe that the Russian authorities were already preparing for the influx of foreign visitors for the 2018 football World Cup and so were introducing bilingual signage and announcements.

The journey was smooth, comfortable and fast, at up to 160 kilometers per hour, with the carriage air conditioned but the outside air temperature flashed up on the information screen as being 26C. I gazed out of the carriage window, noticing in the Moscow suburbs many construction sites with their tall tower cranes for an increasing number of tower blocks, and also the increasing number of new Orthodox churches, due, June had told me, to funding from the Russian oligarchs. As we went along people outside seemed at various points to be using the train tracks as a walkway with no separating fencing lining the route and separating the tracks from fields. They may have been going to and from the numerous dachas. Elsewhere the countryside was covered in trees as far as the eye could see. The journey to

Vladimir took about an hour and a half, held up at times by engineering works.

As already mentioned Vladimir was founded in 1108 by the Kievan Rus Prince Vladimir Monomalch and became the capital of his principality. However, in 1157, under his grandson, Andrei Bogolyubsky, the capital transferred to Suzdal. Vladimir has the ancient Assumption Cathedral, construction of which began in 1158, the smaller Cathedral of St Dmitry built in the late tenth century, these being among the oldest church buildings in Russia, and the Golden Gate, built by Andrie Bogolyubsky, a city gate modelled on that in Kiev which was, in turn, modelled on one in Constantinople. In 1238 the city of Vladimir was overrun and devastated by the Mongols after which it declined and became dependent on Moscow, never to regain its previous status. Nowadays it's an industrial centre but the historic areas are a UNESCO World Heritage site.

On arrival at the ugly, modernist Vladimir train station I knew from my maps and Google earth which way to head for my hotel, the Hotel Vladimir, which used to be a state-run hotel. I found the four storey classical style 1950s building without difficulty and walked in. Again, I handed over my passport to the receptionist to be photocopied. This hotel was my major expense during the trip and on the spur of the moment I decided that I didn't want to use up too much cash paying for this but to keep that in hand. Therefore, I paid with my travel cash card which worked well. Having paid I was shown to my ensuite single room at the front on the first floor. This was clean but was a Soviet throw back with beige walls, a blue carpet and curtains and lots of brown formica panelling, all worn. Further, there was no opening window but some ancient form of air conditioning which hummed. I showered in the dated ensuite, chained my luggage to the bed out of sight of the door and headed downstairs. As I went out I had a chat with the young man at reception and asked if he could 'phone the accommodation I had booked in Suzdal through Booking.com to check that they were expecting me the next night. He entered the 'phone number I gave him and as the 'phone rang he handed the receiver to me but I quickly said 'Nyet Russki' so he conducted the conversation and confirmed that I was booked in there. That was a relief to me and eased my anxieties. He kindly gave me the price of a taxi to Suzdal but my plans had been otherwise laid.

In Vladimir all of the principal tourist sights are on the main street so I strolled up this to the massive Golden Gate with its rounded towers and chapel above and set in the centre of a roundabout, noting the two life sized statues of Red Indians with head dresses standing outside a nearby shop, why I never worked out, and then went back up the hill to the white walled hemispherical domed Assumption Cathedral and the Cathedral of St. Dmitry, with the dome to the Assumption Cathedral topped with a thin pointed spire and the multiple other domes topped with large crosses. The walls to the cuboidal St Dmitry Cathedral were covered at their upper levels with masses of ancient carvings to the stones. These cathedrals are set back from the road with gardens around, the trees painted white at low level against termites, and, as I have indicated, are among the oldest buildings in Russia, dating from the very early middle ages. As I viewed these I kept out of the way of some wedding parties and admired the view across the wooded river valley to the ugly train station and a power plant, and above which a motorized paraglider was circling. Back on the main road I tried to see the Nativity Monastery through the closed gates in the high outer wall but failed.

I moved on to investigate some of the back streets and came across a small church building that was less well kept than the cathedrals. Here a barking dog, fortunately tied up, encouraged me back onto the main road where an old lady was standing in a doorway trying to beg, a fairly common sight in Russia.

Before going on to McDonald's for my evening meal, which Google had told me was present in the main street and which I had now seen with my own eyes, I went down to the bus station, situated next to the train station and of the same ugly architectural style. I looked at the bus stops and found a couple labelled 'Suzdal' and then went into the building to see how I bought a bus ticket, whether from the ticket office or the driver. Standing at the ticket window the clerk and I didn't understand each other and as we were miscommunicating I overheard the group of waiting passengers talking loudly and saying among themselves 'Germaniya?' 'Amerikanskiy?' Velikobritaniya?' 'Gollandiya?'. I almost congratulated the man who got the right nationality for me but in the end kept quiet. I had found out the information that I wanted, that is, that tickets were bought at the ticket window and not on the bus but the cost and times escaped me. I decided that I would have to sort that out the next day.

Now in McDonald's I placed my order - I knew I could order a McDonald's in Russian since 'Big Mac' translates as 'Big Mac' - and the lady supervisor was very good to me and explained in loud Russian, not a word of which I understood, but her gesticulations said it all, that the order number on my receipt would show up on the screen suspended above the counter when my order was ready for collection. I knew the system already but played the game and uttered 'spaseba' a few times and was prepared for when my number appeared.

My family tease me for my love of McDonald's. This is only a love that came out first when I was on this trip and it is not something that I indulge in at home. There are good reasons for that love. Eating in a restaurant is a social activity whereas it is quite acceptable to eat in a McDonald's alone. All McDonald's are similar and are a known quantity and follow the same corporate design and have a familiar fairly inexpensive menu, are clean, unlikely to give me food poisoning and have decent toilets. Such a known environment is good for my stress management. However, I know that I do need to vary the diet a little bit more when travelling.

After eating I went back to my hotel room, tidied my luggage, tried to text home but failed to do so due to a poor signal, quietly strummed and plucked a few ukulele tunes and then went for a final walk before returning, having a self-made coffee and a few biscuits and then sleep.

I did find throughout the trip that the concentration I was having to put into that made me forget my home stresses and anxieties. I was beginning to unwind and my sleep that night was good, despite the lack of fresh air, the constant hum of the air conditioning and the tolling throughout the night of the bell in the nearby monastery!

I woke up early on the Sunday morning feeling ready for the most challenging part of my adventure and the one I was most uncertain about and hadn't been able to pin down fully before I left home, namely the bus journey to Suzdal and back again tomorrow. Showered, dressed and my bag secured and with time to spare before breakfast at eight o'clock I went to look outside again and find out the bus times. As I walked slowly along the road I could see lots of activity around the Assumption Cathedral with large crowds of people in their smartest clothes, with nearly all the women having covered heads, and groups of yellow robed priests, a couple of soldiers with long ceremonial swords and police milling around and with security barriers erected to close off the main road. A flower garland was in the process of being completed around the main entrance doors to the cathedral and kiosks had been set up, serving food. 'What is this all about?' I wondered.

I took all of this in and then headed to the bus station. A couple of staff were outside the bus station building and I showed them my sign saying 'Suzdal' and they took me to stop number ten. I tapped my watch and they jabbered back to me something in Russian, which was no good for me, so I produced my notebook and they wrote down '9.30, 10.00, 10.30, 11.00 …'. 'Spaseba' I said. That was all I needed. The cost of a ticket I would take as it came.

I went back to the hotel for breakfast, reckoning that whatever was going on at the cathedral would start later. On the way back a man worse for wear with drink started yelling abusively at a black robed priest walking up the pavement. A senior police officer nearby immediately raised his arm and beckoned up the road to two other policemen a little way off who then came at a fast sprint down the street and made short work of taking the drunk into custody.

The hotel breakfast was buffet style, laid out in the large, dated and slightly dim dining room, and was very good with cereals, yoghurt, cooked meats, pastries and tea and coffee. I read as I ate and then, without lingering, went upstairs, cleared my room and signed out. Luggage in hand I walked up to the cathedral. Now, just after nine o'clock, police had lined a route from the cathedral along the road to the Golden Gate about a quarter of a mile away with continuous crowd barriers set up and with many reporters and camera men standing in the road. A police commander went down the route turning around every other policeman, telling them to watch the four-deep spectators and not whatever was going to happen in the street. In the distance, beneath the Golden Gate, was a much larger crowd and many bearded priests dressed in bright yellow traditional robes with long wide sleeves and yellow kalimavkion hats as head coverings. As I stood there watching everything that was going on this larger crowd turned around and began a slow walk towards the cathedral, with crosses and heavily patterned religious banners held by grey uniformed and flat capped policemen accompanying the march, and with a bearded priest in the centre dressed in green robes and a white kalimavkion hat as a head covering. The pressmen spoke into their microphones as camera men were guided backwards before the mass of people as they recorded the event.

I was able to get several reasonable photographs of the procession and then, just as the parade was getting really near, my camera batteries failed. By the time I had fished new batteries out of my pocket and loaded them the front of the parade was past me and continuing through the main doorway into the cathedral. Still, even if I wished to have got better, the photos I did take were adequate. I was to find out later that what I had witnessed were celebrations for the anniversary of the founding of Vladimir and the priest in the green robes was Patriarch Kirill, the head of the Russian Orthodox church. The closeness of the secular authorities to the Orthodox church was very apparent.

With all of the activity now out of sight I grabbed my bag from the ground and headed to the bus station. I successfully bought a ticket to Suzdal at the ticket office window with a kind Russian man queuing with me telling me which of a fifty rouble or a hundred rouble note I needed to give to the clerk. I went to bus stop number ten where a small, probably twenty seat, slightly dirty and shabby but robust looking white painted bus with typical Russian big wheels, to give a good ground clearance, presumably to cope with the winter snow, was waiting. I checked with another passenger that this was going where I wanted and with that affirmed I climbed up the steps and found a worn, plastic covered seat towards the back. Over the next little while more and more passengers joined until the bus was crowded. On time, at 10.30, the driver, religious picture swinging from its chain around the rear view mirror, started the diesel engine and with a chugging noise we set off on our forty five minute journey. I was on my way to the place that would be the climax of this trip to Russia!

SUZDAL

THE BUS TO SUZDAL was following the route I had seen on Google earth and on maps before I left home and that was reassuring for me as we went along. I gazed out of the bus window, seeing the domes of Vladimir gleaming in the distance but getting smaller as we left them behind. The road took us through fairly flat agricultural land until we turned left at a roundabout and off the highway and into Suzdal bus station, basically a hard standing and a small office building, on the edge of the town about a mile from the centre and where a couple of long-distance coaches were resting. Many passengers disembarked but I stayed on with a few others. My understanding was that the bus would continue into the town centre. I needed to ask the question to confirm that and tried to do so with one person with some pointing to my map. I wasn't understood but then a young Hungarian girl passenger, probably in her early twenties and who, she told me, had visited London and now lived in Russia, translated my question from English into Russian and relayed the answer back to me 'Yes. It does go to the centre and in a moment the driver will come and collect an extra fare'. I was in awe of her linguistic abilities. Shortly after the driver did indeed come round and collect a few roubles from each of those who remained onboard including my translator and off we went into the town centre, eventually stopping by the trading arcade.

As we left the bus the Hungarian girl and the friend she was with, both on a day trip to Suzdal, asked if I was travelling alone and I explained that I was since this sort of trip was not my wife's idea of fun. As I got my map out again they enquired whether I had accommodation and I thanked them for their concern and assured them that I knew which way to head for that. Or so I thought. I left them behind and started looking for the road I wanted but it just wasn't there. I asked a lady for help but she spoke no English. Looking around I picked a road heading in roughly the right direction and then found an English speaker who confirmed that that road went over the town's river, the river Kamenka, which was where I wanted to be. I later discovered that the road I originally intended to take was a rough back alley and seemed to head over the river by means of a two plank wide walkway with no handrails! I was glad I found another road that took me to my hotel, actually a bed and breakfast, the Dom Alekseyevskaya, half a mile further on at the back of the town. When I was booking I looked at several accommodation options including the Soviet holiday complex through the town and a distance on the other side but the hotel I found was better located. When I at last got there I found that it was a pleasant looking chalet-style building which I easily recognised from the Booking.com photographs.

I booked in at the reception counter, paid in cash, had my passport photocopied and put that away in my belt bag but as I was shown to my room it somehow fell onto the floor. I must have missed the pocket for it and would need to be a lot more careful. Some things I could lose but my passport I could not. In my room I had a quick coffee with my kettle element and mug that I had brought with me and then secured my luggage and headed straight out and into the bright sunshine.

To repeat my previous summary of Suzdal's history, this town is the 'jewel in the crown', the glistening must-see place in the Golden Ring. The town was a royal capital city when Moscow was still a small, insignificant riverside settlement. The first written reference to Suzdal dates from 1024. The city prospered but was destroyed by the Mongols in the late thirteenth century. However, it was re-established and under Ivan the Terrible became a major monastic centre, all such monasteries being fortified. At one time there was a church for every twelve of its citizens as well as fifteen monasteries and even now it remains crammed with churches and monasteries. It became a major commercial centre and its early nineteenth century trading arcade survives. In the later nineteenth century it was bypassed by the

Trans-Siberian Railway and thereafter fell into decline.

I had planned what I was intending to do that afternoon, which was all of the major sites. Suzdal is still filled with walled monasteries but I had chosen to visit only the three largest. The remaining time the next morning I would keep for a general and gentle stroll around.

With determination I set off towards the white painted high walled Pokrovsky Monastery with its Intercession Cathedral and Convent. The cathedral had onion domes but with a very plain interior, as well as many timber cabins installed in the grounds within the surrounding walls as accommodation for tourists. A group of elderly ladies were sitting at the entrance gossiping with each other and they made no effort at all to sell the apples they were displaying on a pram and a push chair. They didn't even look at me, far less ask me to buy any.

After spending half an hour or so at this monastery I moved on to the next monastery situated nearby on the other side of the river and within sight of the first. This was the Saviour Monastery of St Euthymius, surround by high brown painted walls and towers. This monastery has a long history, having been built originally in the fourteenth century. Most recently it was where the German generals captured at Stalingrad were taken for interrogation. Souvenir kiosks lined the approaches to the entrance and I browsed these and bought some small items to take home before paying the entrance fee and going through the huge gatehouse into the complex. There were many buildings inside, including a church with green onion domes on each corner and a golden one in the centre and with highly decorated walls inside, as well as a bell tower, refectory building and even a prison. After spending well over an hour there I made my way down the main road to the white walled Monastery of the Deposition of the Holy Robe, founded in 1207, again with a sixteenth century cathedral within. This was empty of visitors and staff and had not been fully renovated as the others had been. The traditional church buildings and perimeter walls were augmented by a huge yellow painted eighteenth century Baroque style bell tower, seventy two meters high, with white trimmings, a tall, thin spire and timber scaffolding at its lower levels. I wandered around taking photos of churches and derelict buildings and the conical towered entranceways and then found a large stone to sit on while I had a breather, some water, a banana and a chocolate bar.

Half an hour later, revived by my break, I set out for the white painted trading arcade where the bus had dropped me off. I spent a while admiring its aisles lined with classical columns and the trading square to the front with many modern stalls covered with umbrellas.

The final site on my list was now nearby. I walked down a gentle hill, passing horses saddled ready for children to ride, to the remains of the kremlin set on the banks and within the loop of the river but with the fortified walls long gone and only mounds remaining. However, a beautiful white painted church with five blue onion domes decorated with gold stars was present together with a white painted green roofed refectory building and the timber church of St Nicholas.

Across the river I could see the Open Air Historic Buildings Museum, so near and yet with no means of crossing the river at that point, except by a couple of planks which I wasn't going to risk, so far away. By now my feet were aching but I forced myself to walk back the way I had come, stopping at some of the churches as I did so and at a shop to buy water, and then took the road bridge over the river, past my hotel and on another half a mile or so to the museum where I could see the outside of the historic buildings, including timber churches, without having to enter, which was fortunate since it was now getting late and it was past closing time.

All of that walk around the town took me over four hours in very hot, sunny weather and during that time I only heard English spoken by one other person, and that with an American accent.

Near my hotel there was a small solitary building housing a general store. There I replenished my water supplies. At last, exhausted, I staggered back to my accommodation, showered and rested my poor feet. There was no guest lounge at the hotel but the basic room I was in was decent and adequate enough with timber plank doors, plastered painted walls and a small table and chair with a television as well as a double bed and with the ensuite shower and wc in a compartment in the corner. After a while I even got used to the light switches operating upside down to what I was used to at home.

I knew that my evening meal would be a do-it-yourself affair since there was no evidence of a café or even a supermarket in the town and the restaurants that I had seen looked expensive. I had prepared myself for that and now had a couple of pot noodles, some fruit scavenged from that morning's breakfast and some custard cream biscuits brought from home. It was not healthy but for one night was alright and along with a coffee I was content and accepted that as the cost of being where I wanted to go but on a low budget.

I tried to rest but at the back of my mind was the fact that I needed to get back to Vladimir tomorrow to catch the return train. I was very anxious about that. I could catch a bus or coach from the edge of town bus station, walking to that or bussing it, but with my ignorance of Russian, and since, from what I had seen, the Suzdal bus station did not appear to be manned or have any regular staff, I was not sure I would get the right bus to the right place at the right time. This played on my mind until I thought 'You know what, I'll ask the hotel how much a taxi would be. I don't need to carry this stress'.

I wrote out some phrases in Russian from my phrase book - 'Monday 08 IX 14 12.00 Taxi to Vladimir. How much will it cost?' and went to the Russian man, who spoke no English, at the front desk for some sort of conversation. He drew a picture of a bus, asking if I wanted Suzdal bus station and I said 'Nyet. Vladimir Voksal' pointing to Vladimir train station on my map. He gave me a price with which I was happy, the equivalent of twenty pounds and after a 'Da, da, OK' from me the taxi was booked. I felt that it was a cowardly decision but a great weight was lifted from me and it was definitely the right thing to do. I returned to my room relaxed and stress free.

As the evening went on, fairly late by now, I went out again to the Pokrovsky Monastery, only a ten minute walk away, had another look around the now deserted complex, and then as the sun got lower in the sky, it was back to the hotel. I had a text conversation with home, a quiet ukulele session and then crashed out and slept.

The next thing I knew was my alarm clock going off to welcome me to Monday morning. I rolled out of bed, had a good stretch, showered and dressed, secured my luggage and making sure I had a reading book with me headed across the hallway to the small dining room. I was more than ready for the breakfast food spread out on the buffet table - cereal, yoghurts, fruit, cold meats, hard boiled eggs, blinis and jam, fruit juice and coffee. Not being quite sure when I would eat properly again and having a food deficit from the day before I made full use of what was in front of me.

I had not so far seen any other guests but three or four now appeared. However, they spoke something other than English. There was no real conversation between us so I sat, enjoyed reading my book, and ate.

My intention had been to walk around Suzdal again, maybe looking in some more churches, but my feet still ached and it was raining, sometimes a drizzle and sometimes a hard downpour. I used the rain as an excuse to rest my feet and getting wet was certainly not in my plan, especially with few spare clothes packed making a very limited wardrobe in my bag. I stayed in and read and strummed a little but by mid-morning the weather began to clear and I went out around the back streets, exploring a little bit more and seeing some semi-derelict churches. Another large bottle of water was purchased from the general store to replace what I had consumed.

I kept an eye on the time and went back, made sure all my

possessions were packed ready for room check out, sneaked a coffee from the still hot dining room urn, and waited a little while only. Mid-day came and so did a taxi, on time and driven by a youngster with no English. With goodbye said to the hotel's receptionist I put my bags on the car's back seat and myself in the front passenger seat, noting the religious picture on the dash board, and off we went, my driver happily chatting into his hand-held mobile 'phone, as we sped along the road back to Vladimir. Despite the driver's inattention to the road we pulled up intact outside Vladimir train station forty-five minutes later and I paid the agreed price and took my bags.

I was very relieved to be safely back in Vladimir but that gave me a problem. What should I do with the next four hours and with nowhere to leave my luggage?

Entering the station through an airport style security gate and scanner I found a timetable which confirmed my train as the 16.54 with a stop of two minutes but it did not give me a platform number. However, the uniformed lady station manager was very helpful and in sign language and saying 'platform?', which is the same in English and Russian, I found out the right platform and where I needed to stand for my carriage, carriage No 3. I checked my watch and motioned that I would get something to eat to fill the time. In reply she motioned 'do not go anywhere near the food in the bus station café' for which advice I was very grateful and reassured her that I wouldn't and intended to head into town. I used the station wc and then set off to the main road and strolled past all the main cathedrals and sights from the day before. I sat again in the grounds of these and for a second time took in their history. With my feet still aching from yesterday I still made it to the eighteenth century trading arcade nearby before heading to the golden arches of McDonald's for a light snack, a drink and a sit down, this time without the attentions of a supervisor.

Killing time in Vladimir was not very exciting and with hindsight I would probably have done better leaving Suzdal a couple of hours later. However, I was unsettled and keen to make sure I caught the train, remembering the Ekaterinberg incident. I returned to the station at about four o'clock and waited the rest of the time sitting on the platform seats, reading a little, pacing up and down the platform a little, reading a little bit more, looking at the black steam engine monument with its red star on the front and making lists of things to remember to get ready for the next day. At about twenty to five I saw in the distance a red Sapsan train coming from the direction I expected. Was this my train? A couple of hundred yards before the station it stopped and stayed where it was. I kept an eye on it and at the due time it started to move again and slowly made its way along the track to arrive at exactly 16.52, giving two minutes to board. Provodnitsas stood by each carriage door checking documents and tickets and with only a glance at my passport and ticket let me on. At 16.54 the doors were closed and the train sped off, taking me on my journey back to Moscow Kursky station.

MOSCOW AGAIN

AS THE TRAIN PULLED out of Vladimir and sped along the tracks I settled into my soft, comfortable allocated seat and looked at the film picture showing on the screen on the back of the seat in front, thinking that this really was luxury travel. An earphone jack was available for each seat but I didn't have earphones and wouldn't have understood the speech on the film even if I had and could hear it.

I arrived back at the Katerina hotel very relieved to have completed the most adventurous part of my trip. Having been rebooked in with a different room, this time an ensuite single, I went back to reception and e-mailed home, then popped out for a McDonald's, fully aware that I mustn't get used to such bad living, and as I ate a Big Mac I sat and worked out questions for the hotel reception to translate into Russian for me for tomorrow's expedition such as 'Please may I have a return ticket to Sergiev Posad?' and 'Please can you tell me when to get off for Sergiev Posad?' and 'Which platform is the train to Sergiev Posad?'

Food finished I found my way to the Moskva river and watched a lone fisherman on the embankment trying for a catch, made my way past one of Stalin's Seven Sisters skyscrapers situated on the opposite bank and then over Bolshoy Moskvoretsky bridge past St Basil's Cathedral and into Red Square, with barriers and tiered seating and a stage being prepared for a show. I looked around the GUM store and, as it was beginning to get dark as the sun went down returned, showered, texted home, had a strum and then slept soundly. That was until 4am when some sort of noise disturbed me and made me open my eyes but fortunately the call of sleep proved stronger.

The hotel breakfast the next day, Tuesday, was satisfying and again I took full advantage of everything offered as I sat and read one of the hotel's English language newspapers. I took my time to get out of the hotel and into my day, waiting for the morning rush hour to pass. As I waited I approached the reception staff, who spoke good English, and found that they were very happy to translate my phrases for me.

Gathering all I would need for the day from my room - a bottle of water, map, reading book, phrase book, umbrella and spare camera batteries - I left the hotel with confidence that I would be successful in getting to my destination. In the warmth of the day's sunshine I took my well-travelled route to Paveletskaya metro station and now, being a seasoned Russian commuter, confidently headed with my pass onto the platforms, emerging above ground at Komsomolskaya metro station. I knew from my previous reconnaissance with June which way to head for Yaroslavsky main line station.

The day was getting hot as I stood patiently in the queue to the ticket office window. Once at the front I showed my notebook and translated phrases to the clerk who took the rouble notes I offered and printed out a scruffy bit of paper that looked like a till receipt and then gave me coins as change. I turned away from the window, looked at the bit of paper I had been given and was filled with doubt. What did I have in my hand? Was it a ticket or was it just a till receipt?

I tried to ask someone but whilst the man I approached spoke some English I couldn't make myself understood. For a while I stood in a quiet spot and watched people go through the automatic barriers giving access to the platforms and then decided to check with the barrier attendants. My piece of paper had a bar code and they placed this on a reader for me, handed it back as the gates opened and I was through. It's easy when you know how.

That was one challenge successfully completed. The next challenge was to find the right train on the right platform. I knew from my homework - the Bryn Thomas book - that I needed an electrichka, a local electric train, that terminated at Aleksandrov but none showed on the information board. Finding myself standing next to an older lady I asked again for help, saying to her in an enquiring tone 'Sergiev Posad?' and showing her my large lettered sign and my notebook question. She spoke no English but after glancing at the board and finding nothing she dug into her handbag and magically produced a printed timetable and was able to give me a departure time. I thanked her and eventually the train appeared, listed as being from platform ten. Examining the board I carefully counted the stops and noted that Sergiev Posad was the eleventh.

As I walked to the allocated platform there seemed to be an abundance of staff in brightly coloured bib jackets hanging around and I double checked with one of these that I was about to get on the right train. 'Da' they said. This train was very different to the one the previous day. It was painted the same red but the finishes inside were metal and plastic, the seats were hard wooden benches and it looked very utilitarian and functional. The doors were heavy and manually operated. I looked around, found a seat and settled down and the carriage gradually filled. The train left on time, moving northwards through the Moscow suburbs and passing another commuter train with two young lads train surfing by clinging to the outside end of the last carriage. Youngsters are the same the world over!

As the train went past dilapidated buildings a stream of hawkers began to come through the carriage, all wearing the train company's bibs and with microphones and belt speakers they gave their sales pitch accompanied by demonstrations, trying, with occasional success, to sell their wares which ranged from scissors to tea towels. It was these that I had mistaken for staff on the platform. An older lady sat opposite me and I referred to my translated phrases and asked if she could tell me when we got to Sergiev Posad. She replied with an unintelligible - to me - jabber of Russian, the gist of which I took to be that she was leaving the train before my station but that the two teenage girls alongside her were getting off at Sergiev Posad and would let me know.

I watched the view out of the window as suburbs turned to fields and carefully counted stations. At the tenth, not the eleventh, station the two girls opposite got up and started leaving and looking at the platform sign I could see Sergiev Posad written in Cyrillic with English beneath the Russian. I quickly got up from my seat and followed them off the train, down the platform, across the track and outside the station, with no barriers present. I then stopped and pulled out my home printed map.

The working monastery of Sergiev Posad was founded in 1337 by Russia's patron saint, Saint Sergei Radonezhsky, destroyed by the Tatars and then rebuilt with outer defensive walls and with the present buildings which range from the fifteenth to the eighteenth centuries. The Czar from the late sixteenth to early seventeenth century, Boris Godunov, is buried there and it withstood a siege by the Poles in the late seventeenth century. Peter the Great took refuge there early in his reign when facing a military revolt by soldiers of the streltsy guard. The monastery gave its name to the town, although in communist times that was called Zagorsk. The monastery is now a UNESCO World Heritage site and is thought of as a Russian Orthodox equivalent of the Vatican.

Finding the right direction I put my map away and strode off in the heat of the day towards the monastery complex. Soon the golden onion domes became visible and guided me and after only a few minutes I was standing on the monastery forecourt admiring the eight to ten meter high white painted walls with green cappings and huge towers and rising above these from the buildings inside various gold capped baroque bell towers and gold and blue star decorated onion domes.

A sprinkling of people and a couple of tourist coaches were lingering around the open forecourt in front of the entrance. I listened for a while to a lady dressed in traditional clothes playing bell plates but before crowds started to build-up I headed inside. The monastery is a working place of worship and therefore free to enter as are most of the working ecclesiastical buildings in Russia. Many black robed priests with long beards were walking around as well as an increasing number of tourists. I was not on any particular timescale so did not rush but wandered slowly through the many, many churches, the palace and other buildings, some highly decorated, and with many exhibitions. It was a joy to sit every now and then to take in the peaceful atmosphere. Any trip to Moscow should include a visit here.

Having had a good look inside I went out of the entrance gate and set off to my right and did a clockwise circuit around the outside, discovering another church building tucked away at the back on the opposite side of the road.

This had taken a couple of hours and I now needed a rest and a coffee and having checked before I left home I knew there should be a café further up the road. It was further than I expected but it was there, beyond a large and well-kept war memorial. A little while later and much refreshed and with a new bottle of water in my hand I wandered back to the train station, noting as I passed how many more tourist coaches were now parked up outside the monastery. Walking back into the station and onto the platform I found a train standing there, doors open, crowded with many passengers and about to depart in the direction I wanted. Without hesitating I stepped on board and only as the doors shut did I ask 'Yaroslavsky?' 'Da' was the reply gratefully received. I was relieved to hear that but I thought even if not going where I wanted I had time to sort it out and would just have to reverse the journey. My confidence was growing! Each carriage seemed to have its dedicated ticket inspector, accompanied by a security guard and they were content with my ticket. I had to stand all the way back but didn't mind.

Once at the Katerina, having successfully negotiated the metro, I relaxed for a while, very satisfied with what I had done and seen that day. I had a snack from the food that I had brought with me, sadly another pot noodle. At least I had resisted another McDonald's.

Revived I walked up to Red Square again but was tired after the day's excursions and as dusk came got myself back to the hotel and a better snack. Tomorrow was my last day and so it was time to pack and get ready for home. As I did so I realised that I had hardly thought about work for the last few days and the tensions of life had largely drained out of me.

After a good night's sleep I was up on the Wednesday morning at half past six. Showered and dressed I had another very good breakfast in the hotel restaurant to set me up for the day and then, with it still being relatively early and cool, I walked around the block, seeing Moscow come to life, commuters rushing around, cars queuing and sounding horns and all the noises that go with a big city rush hour. There were lots of people heading to and from the metro stations, there were beggars working from their pavement pitches, there were two policemen questioning a couple of swarthy men and checking their papers.

Back at the hotel I booked out and placed my possessions in the hotel's secure store room. Checking that I had a bottle of water with me, since the day promised to be very hot, a promise delivered, I set off back to Paveletskaya and using my pass yet again followed other commuters through the barrier and down onto the platforms. I was catching the metro to Orekhovo, to go to the palace of Tsaritsyno. This palace, set on a hill in the south eastern suburbs of Moscow, was started by Catherine the Great, never finished and left as a shell until 2007 when building restarted and it was completed. When one thinks of Russian palaces the image that comes to mind is something like the decorated palaces in the Moscow Kremlin or the Winter Palace, now the Hermitage Museum, in St Petersburg. This palace is not like those. It is of brickwork with stone ornamentation and is very large with many towers to the elevations. I found my way out of Orekhovo station, the nearest station rather than the station named Tsaritsyno, and up to the palace. I decided not to go inside but enjoyed walking around the large grounds with their fountains and giving views over parkland, lakes and the Moskva river to the wall of high-rise flats, typical of the outer city environs, to the power station in the far distance and in the middle distance to a five onion domed church emerging through trees just beyond the park.

I made my way back to Orekhovo metro station, very glad with my visit to Tsaritsyno Palace but slightly frustrated that I didn't have time to visit the reproduction wooden Kolomenskoye Palace and park of a former royal estate nearby. Time was just too short.

So instead I went through the metro system to Smolenska station, successfully changing at Teatrelnaya to Ploshchad Revolyutsii station, these on different lines but connected as an interchange, with interchanges in Russia not sharing the same station name on each line. From Smolenska I was able to head to the White House, the home of the Russian Duma, Parliament, and which was shelled by tanks loyal to Boris Yeltsin during an attempted insurrection in 1993. Seeing the White House was actually a bit of an anti-climax. Nearby was the modern business district, full of densely packed high rise office blocks and situated on the far side of the Moskva river and reached on foot by a glazed bridge over the river, but only after a fairly long walk along the interesting river bank. I did this walk and climbed the steps up onto the bridge but didn't go further. The business district seemed to be just a modern development. However, the bridge was interesting in itself and worth visiting.

By now I was beginning to tire so made my way back through the metro system to the Katerina, retrieved my luggage, sent an e-mail home from the reception desk and sat in the reception area, resting with a drink.

At about half past four I set off loaded with my luggage for Paveletskaya where I was to meet June who had been working that day. I watched the metro exit and after a little while saw her emerge from the crowds. She had come straight from her school but fortunately was able to travel light with only a small luggage bag.

We had plenty of time to spare so bought some ice creams and chatted away June's stresses of the day. Eventually, checking as always that I wasn't leaving anything behind, a good habit I had got into, we headed into the mainline station. June paused for a few minutes to buy more 'phone credit from a kiosk and then we offered up the bar codes on our tickets and were through the barriers, onto the Aeroxpress train and on our way to

Domodedovo airport.

We had both booked in for our flights online, me before I had even left home, and so, after going through a security check of scanners and metal detector gates to get into the airport, we found a seat and watched the departure boards. All the facilities were on the public side of the boarding gates and we had time to get a drink and a sandwich and that successfully used up nearly all my remaining roubles. We sat and talked and waited. And waited. And waited. No flight information appeared. This was now a familiar scenario for us!

With about an hour to go before departure June went to the Easyjet desk to ask what was happening and came back agitated. Easyjet staff told her they knew the gate hadn't been shown and were telling passengers the gate number when they dropped off luggage. However, as June explained to them, we were travelling on hand luggage only so how were we to be told?

We gathered our possessions and rushed through the barriers to the gates, through border control with passports duly stamped, only to be confronted with another security process - liquids, electrics and shoes into a tray, gilet, drawstring bag, fleece and belt bag into another tray, hand luggage bag and ukulele into a third, check pockets for anything metal, send trays through the scanner, person through the metal detector gate, dress on the other side and seize bags and other possessions out of the trays - and then we ran down the corridor. We arrived out of breath and very stressed with ten or so minutes to spare. Why does it always happen to us?

Easyjet hostesses welcomed us on board and the take-off was on time and smooth. June and I were in different parts of the plane from each other but this wasn't crowded and I had a row to myself so once airborne June came and joined me and I let her have the window seat. She was relieved to move from where she was since she had shared her row with a young couple in love and she said it was all getting a bit yucky!

As we arrived over the United Kingdom in the dark we admired the pretty lights on the ground and soon we were able to pick out towns, then individual roads and then each building and vehicle. The landing was smooth, eyes open this time, and with no hand luggage to collect we were quickly through border control and the customs green channel. It was time to go our separate ways, me to the train station via the airport shuttle, June to catch a bus to Reading where her sister would pick her up to take her to the family home in Swindon. I gave her my best wishes for her father's health.

I caught a fast train to East Croydon then, at East Croydon, with it being very late and feeling absolutely shattered, I decided to take the easy option to get home and so got a black cab from there to my front door. The roads at that time of night were empty but the taxi driver dawdled the whole way and I watched the fare clock tick steadily upwards. As the cab pulled up outside home I had to 'phone my wife to bring out more money for the fare and with hindsight I should have refused to pay and taken the driver's licence number and reported him. However, I was too tired to care but I determined never ever to use a black cab again and I haven't.

As I chatted to my wife for a while I reflected on a good trip, rejoicing that I had coped with the challenges that self-organising posed but realising that I needed to sort out a better eating regime for my next trip - yes, there would be another - and that staying in more than one place is very stressful, too stressful, and also with an awareness that hotels are too isolating for me as a lone traveller. I knew that my mental health would have wobbled badly if June had not been around. Nevertheless, it was so good to have gone. I learned a lot about Russia past and present, about myself, my limits and about travelling, my confidence grew in every way, and for a time I had forgotten the stresses of work and life and focused on other things.

I knew that I would willingly and eagerly do it all again.

AN ADVENTURE TO ST PETERSBURG

TRAVEL TO NEW RUSSIA

ST PETERSBURG

BALTIC SEA

OZERKI

PETERHOF

TSARSKOE SELO

PAVLOVSK

VELIKY NOVGOROD

165km ↓

GOING HOME

SOME MAY CONSIDER ST PETERSBURG to be old but compared to most cities it is not. St Petersburg was founded by Peter the Great in 1703 on disease ridden swamp land at the mouth of the river Neva, one of the most unsuitable places in which to locate a city. However, Peter wanted access to the Baltic Sea, made war on Sweden, who at that time occupied the southern shores of that sea, eventually defeated them and so gained what he wanted. The swamp land was drained by thousands of peasants, the serfs, huge numbers of whom died of disease and maltreatment in the process, and the city was built. Peter the Great moved Russia's capital from Moscow to this new city, building a palace for himself, the Winter Palace, with other palaces built by and for his close associates. The city was founded as an imperial city, a window for Russia onto Europe, and became a major trading and industrial centre. In order to show that Russia had changed, and was no longer an insular backward nation, western ways were forced by Peter onto the Russian ruling classes and onto the church including the banning of Byzantine onion domes within his new capital. As an imperial city it was the place where the Russian revolutions started, the failed Decembrist rising of 1825, the failed 1905 uprising and the successful February 1917 revolution followed by the October 1917 Bolshevik revolution. The Bolsheviks demoted the status of the city by moving the capital back to Moscow.

Whilst Peter the Great's new capital city started life as St Petersburg its name was changed on the outbreak of the First World War in 1914 to the less Germanic sounding Petrograd. The communists changed the city name again in 1924 to Leningrad and then there was another change in 1991, on the fall of communism, back to St Petersburg.

Any serious exploration of Russia must include St Petersburg and I had not yet been there. It was a box I had to, and really wanted to, tick and I would do it 'Clare-style' rather than an organised tour. After my travels 'Clare-style' around Moscow and the Golden Ring a couple of year's previously I knew I could travel in that fashion, needing, of course, to take on board some valuable lessons from that previous trip, and yet still with great trepidation at the prospect of doing so.

I had stayed at home in 2015, a busy year domestically including a breakdown of my health followed after recovery by starting a new job - at last! By the end of that year my life had settled into a new rhythm and subsequently my anxiety levels reduced, mentally I strengthened and my confidence had grown. So now was the time to set off again, the time to dust off my Lonely Planet and Bryn Thomas books and reread these and other books which I borrowed from my local public library - the Bradt book, The Rough Guide, the DK Eyewitness Travel book, Lonely Planet's book dedicated to St Petersburg and any others on which I could lay my hands. Evenings disappeared as I read and reread these but I was immediately confronted with the issue of scope.

Did I want to go just to St Petersburg or also visit places relatively nearby such as Veliky Novgorod? This is an historic city which was founded as a Varangian settlement in 859 and was a principality of Kievan Rus. It became a large independent city state until annexed by Muscovy in 1477 and has a UNESCO World Heritage kremlin site. And what about Pskov, another ancient city with a kremlin and a long history and the place where the last Czar, Nicholas II, abdicated? Was this a possibility? Then there was Vyborg, an historic port city near the border with Finland.

However, eventually, I remembered and paid attention to my last experience and the stresses of moving from one place to another. So, as I looked into the practicalities of travelling around Russia, particularly to Pskov and Vyborg, I cut those from my plans. It would just be too stressful. Nevertheless, Veliky Novgorod was a possibility.

My other concern was to guard my mental health, which was

stable but would need to be looked after and a social environment and a limited length of time in which to be away from home would be best. That concern, as well as budget, led me to investigating tourist hostels. I had come across these before and many years ago as a family we had stayed in a family room in one in Oxford run by the Youth Hostel Association. I had generally thought of them as a younger person's thing but why not older as well? So I went on Booking.com and had a look at the displayed photo wall compendium of several. I was sufficiently impressed that I drew up a shortlist of those in St Petersburg.

Next I tried to put a programme together of what I wanted to see. Top of the list was Tsarskoe Selo, Tsar's Village, a complex of palaces at the town of Pushkin, just south of St Petersburg. Peter the Great's palace at Peterhof was another 'must see' as well as the Hermitage Museum in St Petersburg city centre, a part of which is the Winter Palace. The Peter and Paul Fortress in the city and the Pavlovsk Palace just further south than Pushkin, Orabaum Palace to the west of St Petersburg and Veliky Novgorod also featured. Then there were further sights to see within St Petersburg itself such as the Yusupov Palace, Chesme Church and many, many more. Also, I wanted to be there for the ninth of May Victory Day celebrations and parades which would probably occupy a whole day.

What should I do? The answer was easy. Slim it down. After looking into getting to Veliky Novgorod I realised that this would need an overnight stay and knowing the stresses that jumping accommodation gave me on my last trip I crossed that idea through. That left me staying for the whole time in St Petersburg and then doing very feasible day trips out to the Peterhof, Tsarskoe Selo and Pavlovsk Palace and Park. I thought a week should be adequate to do these and the sights within the city. As I reflected on that I was content. I was in my comfort zone but just pushing that a little at the edges. That was where I wanted to be. Now for the practical arrangements.

The first practical thing to do was to renew my passport, the old one expiring the coming February in 2016. Also, I needed to get some idea of cost. Yet again I spent a couple of evenings browsing the internet and doing sums. Yes, I could afford to go the way I intended. When to go was fixed by wanting to be there on the ninth of May. May also is a good month in terms of weather and temperatures. How long to go for was led by what I wanted to see and as above a week seemed good.

So with my new passport eventually delivered to me it was time, in early February 2016, to start booking 'Clare-style'. First booked were flights with British Airways, then accommodation at Friends Hostel in the very centre of the city by Kazan Cathedral, then insurance with Direct Line and then I went back to JGR for the visa, who used the name 'Stress Free Visas' and again changed my form. This time there was a slightly a different process.

A diplomatic ruckus between the West and Russia meant that finger prints now had to be taken for a Russian visa and so, along with a group of ten or so other people, I met a JGR representative outside an office in Goswell Road in London's Clerkenwell district, this being the office of the Russian Visa Application Centre who handled visa applications for Russia. I was given my visa form to sign together with the return of my passport and then, having been searched by security at the door, processed into the office to hand in the visa application, to pay and to place my fingers on a scanner to record my prints. A couple of weeks later I returned to the same office with my receipt to collect said passport with visa inserted.

Somewhere in that mix of activity I remembered to get my wife's 'approval' and with that achieved I was going to Russia again, this time, finally, at last, more excited than fearful.

As the date for departure approached I went through my usual preparations. I got roubles in low denominations from Marks and Spencer's, with them offering the best rate, then went to the Post Office to secure a travel cash card for my emergency money, in sterling so I could just withdraw remaining money without commission from a cashpoint machine once returned. I put credit on my pay-as-you-go 'phone, checked that my vaccinations were still valid, which they were, made sure I had plenty of camera batteries, bought a few souvenir London fridge magnets to give away, put together a folder for each day with large lettered signs and got myself a small seven inch Acer tablet so I could have internet access and to help keep in touch with home by e-mail. This proved to be a really good and useful purchase. Another good buy was an insulated travel mug. I got a map of St Petersburg from Stanford and printed off maps from Google for Pushkin, Pavlovsk and the Peterhof and then prebooked tickets for the Catherine Palace and the Hermitage. I prepared a list of alternative hostels in case Friends Hostel wasn't as I expected. Then knowing how much stricter airlines were getting with hand baggage I reviewed carefully and ruthlessly what I needed to take with me. One thing I would have to do was to reduce the food I packed and learning from my last airport experience I didn't fill my drawstring bag this time but kept this to separately carry electrical items and liquids as well as documents to help at the airport and with space left in my luggage bag to receive these once through airport security. Leaving my ukulele behind was never an option. Then, as soon as allowed, I booked in online and printed off the boarding card. I left a copy of my programme and contact details and so on with my wife and with that done I was all set to go, nervous but ready.

My flight from Heathrow was not until 9.20am so on Wednesday 4th May 2016 I had a quick breakfast and was then waved off from home in the early hours, while it was still dark, catching the night bus to East Croydon and then just after 5am the fast train to London, a tube train to Hammersmith and then on what I thought would be a final tube train on the Piccadilly Line to Heathrow. The journey was going very well until a ripple of tension ran through the many passengers, luggage indicating that they too were heading for the airport, as the driver announced that the train was terminating at Northfields station, six stops short of

Heathrow. Despite the driver telling us all that another train would be along shortly no-one really believed him and there was a great reluctance to leave the carriages. Nevertheless, the driver was right and whilst the first train was still in the station another pulled in on an adjoining platform and with a palpable sigh of relief everyone quickly crossed over, jumped into the new train, luggage, more luggage, children and all, and not long after we were deposited at our final airport destination.

Once there I followed everyone else across the platform and up the escalators and headed into the Terminal Five departures area. I placed my boarding card on the screen to the entry gate and absolutely nothing happened. I retried without success. I sighed but fortunately the uniformed man overseeing the barriers then came and checked my documents - boarding card, passport and visa - and was happy with those and let me through. Hurdle one successfully jumped. Then it was hurdle two - security. So gilet, fleece and belt bag off and into a tray, liquids and electrical items out of the drawstring bag and into a tray, hand luggage bag and ukulele into a tray, a check of my pockets for any forgotten metal items, then all trays onto the conveyor belt and through the scanner and me through the detector gate and then gilet, fleece and belt bag back on, liquids and electrical items retrieved and into the drawstring bag but with no hand luggage bag and the ukulele tied to this appearing. That was being held by a lady security officer who called me over.

'Here we go again' I thought. The lady, a nice lady, explained that my bag was too tightly packed for the scanner to see what was in there. So I unlocked it for her and she undid all my careful packing, was happy with what she found, or rather didn't find, and then left me to repack. As I did so I squeezed in my liquids and electrical items.

I had time to relax and recover from the journey so far. After checking the departure boards and gate locations I had a coffee, ate my carefully packed pastries as a second breakfast and also bought two bottles of water ready for arrival in St Petersburg. As

I waited I went to send a text home but had a problem. My 'phone had somehow gone onto predictive text and however much I tried I could not reset it. What to do? I 'phoned my daughter but she was absolutely no help at all. I thought youngsters were the experts! I asked the man sitting next to me who didn't know and so I settled down to searching the different menus and after some considerable time managed to fix it. That was a great relief - I would need my 'phone to communicate with home throughout my trip - and a text message was eventually sent.

All was straight forward getting onto the aeroplane with passport and boarding card checked, a smile exchanged with the stewards and my bag placed in the overhead locker within sight of my allocated seat. Passengers kept boarding, more and more, until the aeroplane was full, the doors were closed, seat belts and chair arms checked, the safety 'dance' performed and we were off. I was braver this time and kept my eyes open for take-off and had a splendid view of Windsor Castle from my window seat as we ascended. Attempts at conversation with the passenger next to me failed but the flight of the A320 Airbus was without issue and as we flew over the coast of Holland I saw colonies of windfarms. As we crossed over Denmark a good breakfast of scrambled egg and hash browns was served.

After three hours the 'Fasten Seat Belt' sign came back on and as the plane descended I gazed out of the window again and admired the golden domes on the churches below, noted Pavlovsk Palace appearing beneath and then we flew over numerous large blocks of flats in the St Petersburg suburbs. The landing at St Petersburg's Pulkovo airport was smooth, hardly a bounce, and with completed landing card in hand I waited patiently, unlike other passengers, for the plane to taxi, gantries to be fixed, doors opened and disembarkation to commence before retrieving my bag from the overhead locker. Then it was through border control - 'Purpose of visit?' 'Tourism', stamp in passport, barriers opened - then customs and then I marched past the taxi driver mob to where I was expecting the E39 bus to be, which it was. This would take me into St Petersburg. I paid the driver, using coins kept over from my last trip to Russia, found a seat and after a little while the bus set off into busy traffic and headed for the city. I was familiar with the route from following this on Google earth and so recognised the Ploshchad Pobedy, Victory Square, roundabout with its distinctive Heroic Defenders of Leningrad war memorial and adjoining tower blocks by which I knew that we were near to Moskovskaya metro station where the bus terminated. Now at its destination the bus emptied and I stood on the pavement breathing in Russian air and gazing at the white, blue and red banners, with hammer and sickle emblems, hanging across the road ready for the Victory Day celebrations. Before heading into the metro station I checked the location of the bus stops for the journey back to the airport, essential knowledge for when I came to depart for home. As I looked around the street with its Cyrillic signs and Stalinist buildings all seemed very familiar and I felt that I had returned home. That was fanciful rubbish of course!

Going through the entrance doors into the metro station I acted like a local and approached the ticket office window and held up ten fingers for ten journeys, paid and received ten tokens. Before going any further I stowed nine of these safely away for future use and then walked across the foyer and slipped the tenth into the gate which allowed me to walk through without closing. I had checked my metro map and knew which destination station, Nevsky Prospect station, I wanted and didn't have to change lines at all but just pick the right direction. Thankfully I did and seven stops later I walked off the train and onto the very, very big up escalator, so big that the top was not visible from the bottom. The St Petersburg metro is extremely deep, having been built beneath the bottom level of the area's marshland, and also to provide shelter in the event of nuclear war, with the platforms to this station being sixty-three meters down. After many, many minutes I reached the top and was discharged onto Nevsky Prospect with Kazan Cathedral opposite on the other side of the Griboyedov canal.

As I stood in the hot sunshine I was glad that I had got this far and knew that the Friends tourist hostel was nearby. I looked out my large lettered address sign and successfully crossed the Prospect at pedestrian lights without getting run over and strolled the fifty yards to where I thought the hostel should be. There were no name signs on the street identifying it and no building numbers. With increasing nervous apprehension I walked up and down the road with no joy and in the end went into a café on the other side of Nevsky Prospect, having, again successfully, recrossed that, and showed someone the address I was after. They puzzled over it for a few minutes and then directed me back the way I had come. This time, when I thought I was near, I was brave and went into side alleys and through arches to the back space of buildings, and there, at the rear of a building opposite the Cathedral but separated from that by the canal, and off a courtyard full of parked cars and bicycles, was the name plate that I had been looking for, small but nevertheless adequate, saying 'Friends Hostel' with an arrow pointing to a purple painted solid, closed, metal clad door. So it was secure then.

I rang the bell next to the door. Nothing. I rang a second time and a voice came to me through the intercom saying things I didn't understand. However, there was a buzz and I opened the door, which was as heavy as it looked. I stood in the blue decorated stairwell and the only way I could go was upstairs and eventually, two landings up, there was an office window and someone waiting for me to get my breath back and book me in. Apart from the cost of the accommodation I had to pay a charge for passport registration with the authorities, for linen and for a deposit for my locker key which also had a fob for the outside entrance door. None of the charges was great. The receptionist, Veronica, asked if I wanted to book a breakfast for the next day and I thought that would be good and that was another charge. That all done she showed me to the green painted laminate floored six bed, that was three sets of bunk beds, all male dormitory with a top bunk allocated to me. I was shown my good-sized locker, and then the toilets and showers and the reasonably equipped kitchen with kettle, microwave and all the necessary cutlery and crockery. We returned to my dormitory and I was then left to my own devices. I had arrived and I could now relax. It was a lovely feeling.

I looked around. Everything was clean and functional but a little worn. The window looked out over other buildings and it was a shame it didn't have a view of Kazan Cathedral but I wouldn't be spending time in the room looking out of the window anyway. I secured my bag in the locker and headed to the windowless kitchen with a bottle of water, my insulated mug and my kettle element and made myself a coffee, deciding not to use the provided kettle or water. That was because I couldn't work out whether the supplied kitchen water was drinkable. I decided to keep clear of it and use my own bottled water, remembering the advice of a good friend who suffered for years after contracting a water borne infection abroad and who told me 'not even for cleaning your teeth!' An upset stomach was the last way in which I wished to spend my time in Russia so I followed that advice. Coffee in hand I relaxed at the kitchen table, had a few of my own biscuits, and gathered my thoughts. Then finishing my coffee I took out of my bag and then threw away the bunch of three bananas I had brought with me from London. I thought that they would be good for me and they would have been but just didn't survive the journey and were now black and inedible. I made a note for future reference. Finally, I returned to the dormitory, secured my things in my locker and went outside into the afternoon sunshine.

Standing on the pavement I looked ahead to Kazan Cathedral and looked to my right to the Church of the Saviour on Spilled Blood and to the iconic Singer Building. However, I didn't head for any of those. Instead I headed over the Moyka river towards Palace Square. I wanted to check out the hydrofoil station at Palace Bridge behind the Winter Palace. I had decided to do my more stressful 'out of town' visits first, to the Peterhof the next day and then to Tsarskoe Selo the day after and then to Pavlovsk the day after that, before using the rest of the time for sights within the city. The hydrofoil would take me to the Peterhof since I had decided that was the easiest route to take, more so and more fun than taking the train, the nearest train station to the palace being about one and a half miles away from that. Ironically, as events would show, I never contemplated taking a bus - I could end up anywhere!

I found the hydrofoil station, checked the price and sailing times and then strolled along the main frontage of the elegant green and white Winter Palace, brown embellishments completing the scene, and found the entrance to the Hermitage Museum that I would need later in my stay, and then went across Palace Square, with its yellow and white painted classical military buildings opposite the Palace and its Alexander Column celebrating the Russian defeat of Napoleon, before going through the large arch and back into Nevsky Prospect by the Stroganov Palace. Strolling along the canal side I had a closer look at the Church of the Saviour on Spilled Blood, situated on the site where the reformist Czar Alexander II was assassinated, and with its many very brightly coloured onion domes sending a reactionary statement to the city. I browsed the various tourist souvenir kiosks and immediately bought some fridge magnets as souvenirs and then walked a little way, crossed the road and went through the huge double doors of Kazan Cathedral with its columned cloisters mimicking those of the Vatican's St Peter's and extending like arms towards the street. Inside it was poorly lit and my eyes took a while to adjust. I crept around the unfurnished interior with its dome and columns, respecting those worshipping and feeling a compassion for them as they bobbed before icons and kissed them.

Back in the bright daylight I went down the elegant Nevsky Prospect with its many fine buildings, all low rise, as far as my legs would take me, as far as the Ploshchad Vosstaniya with its Leningrad Hero City Oblisk and on the way back into the 1770s Armenian church, its simple interior in contrast to most Orthodox churches. Passing a fast-food outlet in the Prospect I treated myself to a milkshake and then, refreshed, returned towards the hostel. However, I did another circuit past the Church of the Saviour on Spilled Blood, the park behind and Mars' Fields and then, as the sun set, back into Palace Square, taking in another Orthodox church, this time simply furnished, on the way.

It was now early evening and so I had a comfort break at the hostel. I needed to eat and retrieved some of the pot noodles I had packed and sat in the hostel kitchen 'enjoying' these. They were acceptable and adequate for that night. As I sorted out my bag back in the dormitory another guest appeared, Uri, a Russian from near Murmansk, who worked on ships ferrying cars from the Ford car plant at Dagenham over to Amsterdam, and who was in St Petersburg for a couple of days for business meetings with his job.

By now I was tired but it was still a long way from full darkness which at this time of year was after eleven o'clock. With a coffee in hand I went out again and listened to some of the very good street buskers, both bands and solo artists, for quite some time before returning and crashing out for the night, very happy and relaxed, stress and anxiety free.

OUT AND ABOUT

IN THE EARLY MORNING of Thursday I was aware of someone else joining the dormitory with a certain amount of moving around and opening and shutting of the door. I was to find that this was the nature of hostel life with constant comings and goings at all times of day and night. I would go to sleep with one set of people in the room and wake up with a completely different set of people. However, those comings and goings didn't disturb me for long and I slept well until my 'phone alarm, set to go off very quietly, beeped at about 7am.

Showered, dressed and still with time before my breakfast was due to arrive at eight o'clock I went into the clear cool air of a morning that promised to be bright and hot. I enjoyed my stroll when the streets were quieter and went through the nearby Palace Square again before buying essential water supplies at a kiosk and returning to a still sleeping hostel.

At just gone 8am Irina, one of the receptionists, handed me my breakfast package over the reception counter and I wandered into the kitchen to eat it. A good breakfast should set me up for the day with little need for any substantial lunch. However, the breakfast didn't seem very warm and when I opened the lid of the polystyrene box I found that it wasn't. I looked at the microwave, all labelled in Russian, but nevertheless put the package inside, closed the door, took a chance and turned a dial and pressed a button and to my relief it whirred into life. I timed two minutes on my watch, after which my food was definitely hot and went down very well, together with a self-made coffee.

As I ate an American man, Joe, from Florida, who looked about my age, may be a bit older, with his New Zealander wife Debbie, came into the kitchen. They had a double room in the hostel and we had a nice conversation covering whether the water in the hostel was safe to drink, me assuming that it wasn't, and politics including the merits or otherwise of Donald Trump, this initiated by them, and our plans whilst in St Petersburg.

Breakfast finished I packed my drawstring bag with an umbrella, a bottle of water, a reading book, maps and some biscuits from home and went off to the hydrofoil station, a little tense at the prospect of the journey ahead of me. Would I manage to get where I wanted? Once at the station I found a queue already forming and I was disappointed to discover that the first boat with space wasn't until eleven o'clock and then that I could only buy a single ticket, which I did, with the return ticket having to be purchased at the Peterhof hydrofoil office. However, that was actually to stand me in good stead. I now had an hour to spare so joined the queue and passed the time watching the other river traffic and chatting to an also waiting American couple from San Francisco.

Eventually we were able to board the hydrofoil. I would have liked a window seat but they were quickly taken by those at the front of the queue. Nevertheless, the windows were large and I got a good view of the shoreline as the hydrofoil, which seemed to have a number of Palace staff on board as well as tourists, cast off and rose out of the water to speed the half hour journey to the pier at the foot of the Peterhof Palace canal. As we got nearer to our destination I noted the huge Peter and Paul Cathedral, unfortunately surrounded by sheeted scaffolding. I made a mental note to make sure I got a starboard seat on the way back which would give me a second look at the coast line.

Once moored I followed everyone else off the boat and up the walkway to the Palace ticket office. Standing behind two or three other people at the office window I struggled to read the prices in the unclear illuminated display and couldn't make out to what the different costs referred. When I did get to the window I was further flummoxed by not being able to see the non-English speaking clerk on the other side of the dark glass. In the end I gave up trying to ask questions, particularly whether the Lower Park and the Upper Park are on the same ticket - I was to find out that the Upper Park is actually free - and since I had already decided that I only wanted the park - both palace and park I thought would be too long a day - I said 'Park, nyet dvorets' 'park no palace' and got the corresponding ticket.

The Peterhof was originally built by Peter the Great in the early eighteenth century and he expanded the original building after a visit to Versailles and also had the gardens constructed. The palace was further extended by the architect Francesco Bartolomeo Rastrelli for the Empress Elizabeth in the middle of the eighteenth century and now comprises the Palace and gardens with multiple buildings set within these. In the Second World War the palace was captured by the Germans and Hitler intended to use it to hold a victory celebration. To prevent this Stalin ordered the palace to be bombed and destroyed. After the war the communists renovated the complex. It is now a UNESCO World Heritage site.

I approached the Palace with its magnificent fountains and cascade from the bottom of the canal which is overlooked by the palace up on a ridge at its head. It was difficult to get a decent photograph of anything due to the build-up of visitors and later in the day, when the coach parties arrive in force, it must get extremely and unpleasantly crowded. Within the Lower Park, populated by red squirrels as well as tourists, are many lodges and other buildings and these were all interesting as were the photo displays giving the Palace's history. I spent a long, long time in the Lower Park before finding my way up to the back of the site.

I wanted to be able to leave the grounds and have a look at the old and very large palace stable block behind. There was a gate in the perimeter railings at the rear, manned by good humoured security guards and the question I wanted to ask them was whether, if I went out, would I be able to get back in, but the language barrier intervened. In the end, having seen all I wanted to see in the Lower Park, I decided to go out anyway and was able to confirm with the guards my understanding that there was a bus stop to St Petersburg on the main road at the back. Everyone was friendly even though we couldn't understand each other and having thoroughly explored the Lower Park I exited and found the stable block I was looking for. Sadly this was undergoing renovation and was fenced off but with wire fencing so I was able to see the courtyard in the middle and walk all around the outside walls.

From there I went into the Kolonistskiya Park and then to the Peter and Paul Cathedral and had a look inside, the outside, as I noted earlier, being completely obscured by scaffolding, and then I set off along the road to the elegant and free Palace Upper Park before avoiding the numerous tourist coaches and carefully crossing the main road to the bus stop. I had a note from the Lonely Planet book of the buses and marshrutka, that is minibuses, that would take me back to St Petersburg and so long as I ended up at a metro station, any metro station, I would be happy and able to negotiate my way from there back to the hostel.

As a marshrutky pulled up I checked the destination on the front, showed my St Petersburg sign, was ushered on board by the driver who took my cash fare and then I was in his hands. I had no idea where I was going but as we got into the city suburbs I asked the person next to me 'metro?' and she pushed me out at the right stop for a metro station. It wasn't the Leninski Prospekt station advertised on the marshrutky's front as its end point but Avtovo station. A few years ago I would not have been sufficiently brave to jump on a marshrutky and make a journey like this and would have had a meltdown. I marvelled at how much I had changed. I went into the station's ornate entrance foyer, in fact the whole station inside and outside was ornate, with a domed roof and classical columns, and looked for the name on my metro map. Having found it I fished a counter out of my belt bag and went through the barriers and down to the platforms with their mosaic decoration at the end and headed to the Pushkin Square stop, made easier to find by the dual language - Russian and English - signs. On the train police were stopping and searching anyone of darker complexion, maybe Chechens, so being as pale skinned as a local I thankfully didn't get pulled aside for questioning.

Pushkin Square metro stop is the one that serves Vitebsky main line train station and I wanted to have a look at that ready for my planned excursion tomorrow. The station was easy to find but it took me a while to locate the section for the local trains, running on the first railway line in Russia, built in 1837 between St Petersburg and Tsarskoe Selo, later extended to Pavlovsk, and with one of the first trains safely kept behind glass at the station as a museum piece. This local section wasn't part of the main station but a smaller separate station down the right hand side of the other one. I wandered into the local station ticket hall and started looking at timetables. Eventually I worked out and confirmed what I wanted, that is, to get to Tsarskoe Selo I would need to take the train heading to Pavlovsk and that they were every half an hour. The name of the station I needed to get off at no longer went by its previous names of Pushkin, so called after the town it served, and Detskoe Selo. After making some notes to explain what I wanted I had a conversation of sorts with the ticket clerk and she confirmed that I needed the Pavlovsk train and in the end I also understood the single and return fares. With that done I found a cafe and sat and relaxed with a coffee.

Suitably rested but with my feet beginning to ache I followed my map and made a slow walk back to the hostel, stopping at a shop on the way to buy a late lunch - it was tea time by now - which I had in the hostel kitchen with a self-made coffee. As I did so I did a list of what I needed for the next day.

After that I went exploring, across the pedestrian Griffin Bridge over the Griboyedov canal, so called because of the large griffins with golden wings at each end, past St Isaac's Cathedral, looking a bit like London's St Paul's with a hemispherical dome, and then pressed on to the New Holland Complex. This was the site of shipbuilding in Peter the Great's time and on the map it seemed to be interesting with a moat around it but in practice it was a derelict boarded up site waiting to be refurbished. I walked all around the outside with nothing of interest apparent before returning past the Mirinsky Theatre and St Nicholas Cathedral, past rows of parked cars with veterans' ribbons, similar to our memorial poppies, placed beneath the windscreen wipers, and eventually ending up in Nevsky Prospect. On the way I found a basement general store - many such stores are randomly located and nearly always in basements - and bought some cornflakes and milk to supplement my cooked breakfasts.

Back at the hostel there was a new person in the dormitory, fast asleep, so I crept around and quietly put the cornflakes in my locker and the milk, with my name on the carton, in the kitchen fridge and then went out again. Turning into Nevsky Prospect I went over the Fontanka river and treated myself to a McDonald's which I successfully ordered in Russian! I sat reading, holding my book in one hand and getting messy fingers on the other. As I did so a man approached me and in good English asked for money. I turned him down but how did he know I was a tourist and English at that? Was it just from the book I was reading? Later I was approached by another beggar, still in McDonald's, but he spoke only in Russian and I waved him away.

Hunger now abated I popped back to the hostel and made up a coffee in my insulated flask, a purchase that has proved very useful time and again, and then stood in Nevsky Prospect listening to a busker with a dog at his feet and a ukulele in his hand, certainly meriting the coins I put into the hat on the pavement. I then avoided an old lady begging and enjoyed more buskers by the Singer Building including a very good trumpeter standing on one of the canal railing piers, before re-entering the accommodation. As I got my tablet out of my locker the previously sleeping man was up and about and after a greeting and a smile he headed off, presumably for a night on the town. I was alone in the room so had my own ukulele session. I checked my printed out e-ticket for the Catherine Palace at Tsarskoe Selo, the town originally of that name renamed by Stalin to Pushkin, and that was when I discovered that I had somehow booked this for a week ahead rather than the next day. I wondered how that could have happened but did remember that the Palace online booking system hadn't been the easiest to negotiate. I would have to get there early to sort that out. I checked my printed out paper e-ticket for the Hermitage for the day after and thankfully that was correct. Then I took my tablet into the kitchen but struggled to get a signal. After some time and frustration I eventually managed to get one and logged on through the hostel's router. I caught up with e-mails from home including a photo of another just-born grandchild! With that happy news I took myself off and got ready for bed, climbing into my bunk relaxed and content, and fell asleep quickly, despite the half-light still present through the window.

I was up with the lark on Friday morning at about half past six, and without waking anyone else showered, dressed, and had a breakfast with the cornflakes and milk I had bought and then made an early exit from the hostel and walked the route back to Vitebsky station, buying yet another bottle of water on the way. I went to the local station and bought a return ticket to Tsarskoe Selo. I carefully checked the number of intervening stations on the information board so I could count them down, with the one before Tsarskoe Selo having the descriptive name of 21km, and then climbed the steps up to the platform. I managed to pick the right train, heading to Pavlovsk, and climbed on board. The train left on time at 8.25am and as I sat on the hard wooden bench seat in the mostly empty carriage I looked out of the window at the surroundings as they changed from city centre to suburbs to countryside, counted the stations and was pleased when the inspector checked my ticket without comment.

After four stops the station 21km came up which surprised and confused me since I was expecting that to be the seventh station but I checked with one of the few other passengers and got off at the next stop, the correct one. Even though it was early it was already getting very hot and I was glad I had a decent supply of water. I walked around the end of the brick-built station building into the station forecourt and a bus with the right number, as advised by one of the travel books I read but which one I cannot now trace, was waiting and full and seemed ready to go. I stepped on board, showing my 'Ekaterinski Dvorets', Catherine Palace, sign and received a 'da' from the driver. As I moved further down the bus, with standing room only remaining, the doors shut and the bus moved off. I looked for a conductor but there didn't seem to be one so, with the attention of the man standing next to me, I rubbed the thumb and first finger on my left hand together and he pointed to the driver and then to the display showing the amount. At the first stop I paid the driver the right amount and then, mentally picturing the town map, followed the bus route in my mind as we drove on and at the right stop, as I had already seen at home on Google earth, stepped off, with the kind bus driver pointing me in the direction I wanted. 'Spaseba' I said. I was glad that I had caught the bus since the distance from the station to the palace was over a mile.

The bus went on its way and I went on mine and I turned the corner of the street to see a most glorious sight of the palace which words are inadequate to describe so I will not do so. It needs to be seen to be appreciated.

The history of the Catherine Palace starts with Peter the Great giving the estate of Sarskoye Selo to his wife Catherine. This estate subsequently became known as Tsarskoe Selo, Czar's Village. The Catherine Palace was built around 1723, was replaced by the Empress Elizabeth in the 1740s and given a complete overhaul in the 1750s by the architect Rastrelli, resulting in its present blue and white finish with beige dressings and statues. Further extensions were added in the 1770s and in the 1780s the Scottish architect Charles Cameron added a wing. After the Russian revolution Tsarskoe Selo was renamed Detskoe Selo, Children's Village, before returning to its original name with the fall of communism. The palace was intentionally destroyed by the Germans in the Second World War leaving only a hollow shell but not before they had removed the famous Amber Room. This was never found and remains a matter of mystery and intrigue.

Reconstruction of the palace was started by the communists in 1957 and continues to this day with only about a fifth of the palace open to the public with the rest still being under renovation.

My first task when I arrived was to see if I could sort out my e-ticket. Beyond the built-up arch over the road is a timber shed ticket kiosk, next to the side entrance where e-ticket holders go in. It was just after nine o'clock and this kiosk didn't even open until ten o'clock and if my e-ticket had been correctly dated I would have gained access at that time. I pondered what to do. Even if I was able to have a conversation with the ticket clerk I was not at all sure that I would be able to explain my mistake without use of the Russian language I didn't possess, so eventually I decided to abandon the idea of trying to sort out my e-ticket. Instead I took the stress free option and went back through the built-up arch and at the entrance nearby there bought a new ticket for the grounds, being told that tickets for the Palace should be bought at the palace doors. In United Kingdom terms these tickets were not expensive so I didn't mind paying again. I decided to see the grounds first before joining the queue for the Palace which opened at noon to those people not prebooked. I had read somewhere that this queue could be three hours long so I walked around the grounds, not rushing but certainly not dallying, went around the lake, went to the Hermitage Pavilion and eventually joined the line of people waiting for the Palace entry a little after ten o'clock. I was content that abandoning my e-ticket was the right decision. If I had tried to sort out that out and failed I would have then been joining this queue even later.

Unfortunately there was no shade from the hot sun for this queue but I coped with that as did others. Those of us in the line got chatting together. In front of me was a German girl around twenty years old who was spending a year out before university, living in Estonia and helping with educationally slow children as voluntary work. She was spending a few days in Russia having travelled from Tallin by bus and then couch surfing with someone in Pushkin, arranged through some website. Immediately behind me was a tour guide who gave me a card to introduce herself as Svetlana Drozdova from guideforyou-russia.com, holding a place in the queue for four Finnish people, two married middle-aged couples, who were wandering the grounds. The day before she had been taking people around the Hermitage Museum where, since that had been one of the museum's free days, the queue had been four hours long. At least this queue should not be that. However, the guide said that three hours wasn't unusual but it was summer which was good since last year the winter temperature had dropped to minus twenty degrees Celsius and waiting three hours at that temperature would be very difficult.

The Finnish people eventually arrived. They were very pleasant and one couple had lived in the London suburb of Kingston for five years so they knew London well. I did ask them, tongue in cheek, whether Finland was always cold and dark and they said 'No, of course not, it's a lovely country. Is it always raining in London?' to which I could only answer 'Actually, yes. It is always raining in London'. I assured them that I would put Finland on my list of countries to visit. As we waited tour parties would walk past us and straight to the front of us all but we suffered that and at noon the line of waiting people was admitted, with payment made at the entrance which let into the ground floor. Useful toilets were at this level, very useful having stood waiting for a couple of hours, and then I went straight outside to the rear to view that elevation of the Palace. Back inside visitors were directed to the red carpeted stairs up to the first floor where shoes had to be covered with provided polythene slip-ons to protect the polished floor to the Grand Hall. As I went into this large room huge mirrors made it seem even larger and the painted ceiling, the walls covered in gold detailing, the mirrors and the polished floor was a magnificent show of rich luxury that must have impressed all who were invited by the Czars to the palace. Tourists were guided out of the Grand Hall to the other richly decorated and furnished first floor rooms including a fine and highly decorated chapel and the reconstructed Amber Room, completed in 2003 with donations towards this made by the German government. Many of these rooms had full height tiled stoves in a corner. The palace was crowded but not unbearably so. On the way out I bumped into Svetlana and her Finnish group and asked her about the Alexandra Park and Palace behind the Catherine Palace. She told me she thought it was shut but on checking with a member of staff I was told that the park was open and free.

Leaving the Catherine Palace grounds I turned left and went beneath the archway over the road and approached the entrance to the Alexandra Park. This did have a chain across the gateway but was hanging low so I was able to step over that and into the park and found myself in an attractive area of lawns and flower beds. Within the park is the Alexandra Palace which was the preferred home of the last Czar. This palace was built by Catherine the Great for her grandson, the future Czar Alexander I, in the late eighteenth century. After the February 1917 Revolution it became the place of detention for the last Czar and his family. I found this was surrounded by hoardings whilst building work was going on but I sneaked a look at the frontage through a gap in these and walked all around the outside viewing the upper levels. Beyond the palace is the Chinese Village but this was a gated area of smart housing with no access allowed.

My explorations were now finished so I walked out of the park past various derelict buildings and wandered back towards the bus stop, past the Znamenskaya church, the Lycee and the boarded-up Catherine Palace Orangery. I waited for a bus on the opposite side of the road to my arrival stop but suddenly realised that I had no idea what numbers would take me back to the train station except the one I came on. Two or three marshrutka pulled up but I had no sign saying 'Voksal' - train station - and had to let them go. In the end, since it was only about a mile or so and I had a map in my hand I decided to walk, but not fast. After all, the weather was incredibly hot.

I had some time to wait before my train back to St Petersburg was due and so admired the station, in the process of being upgraded, and its beautiful painted ceiling. I got out my camera and took a photograph of this ceiling, to be immediately reprimanded by a uniformed station attendant. I reassured her that I had only photographed the ceiling and showed this to her on the camera and then quickly put my camera into my gilet packet and walked away across the tracks to the plank platform, having now learned, or rather relearned, that lesson. For some unknown reason photographs are acceptable on the metro but not on the overground railways.

The journey from there back to Vitebsk station was straightforward with an intriguing steam engine graveyard, full of rusting relics, on the western side of the railway. On arrival I realised how tired I was and my feet ached. Nevertheless I got the metro from the nearby Pushkin Square, not to the station for the hostel but to Ploshchad Vosstaniya metro station, outside the Moscow Station, a main line terminus, changing lines successfully on the way. This was a bit further down Nevsky Prospect and it would be interesting to walk again up the Prospect from there, despite my feet, and have another look at the graceful buildings situated there. As I left the station a girl was handing out Victory Day ribbons so I took one and pinned it to my gilet. With that on me I was beginning to look like a Russian.

Walking along I went through the tourist stalls both above ground and also in the pedestrian underpasses. I stopped and browsed through the wares and managed to buy T-shirts for the grandchildren, checking sizes against ages with the store keeper and against a photograph of them all. Thanks to a decent exchange rate they were good value.

Further up the Prospect I came to a cafe and called in for a drink and a snack and a rest. As I gathered my thoughts together I decided to change my programme. The next day I was due at the Hermitage and then intended to go down to Pavlovsk Palace. This palace was built in the late eighteenth century by Catherine the Great for her son, the future Czar Paul I, and was again designed in classical style by the architect Charles Cameron. It is set in

English-style park land. After the 1917 revolution it became a museum. The German army set fire to the palace as they were forced out of the area in the Second World War but it was restored by the communists. However, I was palaced-out and not sure my feet would cope with that amount of walking. I decided to leave Pavlovsk for another visit and as the trip went on realised what a sensible decision that was in preventing over-tiredness and its accompanying mental wobbles.

I spent that evening tidying my luggage, sending an e-mail home from my tablet, now with a steady internet connection, and ordering breakfast for tomorrow. I went out and bought some more water and returned to check the blisters on my feet and have a meal from the last of the food I had brought with me. As I did all this an Australian youngster from Sydney joined the dormitory. He was travelling on a gap year and had come by bus from seeing his father in Finland and was heading back there later. He went out and I went into the kitchen to make myself a coffee in my insulated mug and found it full of well-behaved ten-year-old children and their teachers, all busily eating and staying somewhere in the hostel. Coffee made I went out to the park behind the Church of the Saviour on Spilled Blood and read for a while before strolling to the Admiralty Building and its park and then through Palace Square, with its Peter the Great and Catherine the Great lookalikes still working, before finding a good spot to listen to buskers by the Griboyedov Canal on the corner of Nevsky Prospect, with the crowd vigorously joining in with some of the songs. I listened to the voices in the crowd. There were a few Americans, a few Germans but no British voices and the city did not seem to have any great ethnic mix.

This time I stayed out until after dusk to see Kazan Cathedral and the Winter Palace and Church of the Saviour on Spilled Blood floodlit, giving them a beauty of a different emphasis to the daylight view, and so it was late when I eventually returned to the dormitory. I was glad that I had completed those parts of the trip that had made me the most anxious. Satisfied at my successful days so far I crept into bed, quietly, so as not to disturb the sleeping body in the bunk opposite.

THE CITY

FROM THE DEPTHS OF sleep, at about half past six on Saturday morning, I was aware of a trickle down my nose and quickly, and successfully, grabbed the handkerchief I had with me before any blood from my sudden and unexpected nose bleed reached the bed clothes. What a way to wake up. As quietly as I could I made it to the bathroom and sorted myself out. Now awake I had a shower and dressed and I realised that Uri had disappeared at some time in the night. I had a coffee in the kitchen and after a little waiting my good breakfast arrived and by half past eight I was outside in the cool air of what was going to be another hot day.

Walking into Palace Square I was surprised to find it full of soldiers rehearsing for the Victory Day Parade on the coming Monday, with a line of cadets keeping watching spectators confined to one side. There were uniforms of different colours with squads of men and women soldiers being marched about, tanks, including T34s, rumbling around and throwing out huge plumes of dirty smoke, some rocket launchers and cannons being driven in formation, a staff car with its saluting officer, one platoon of blue bereted troops lined up with their guns for a group photo and a band who several times would march off playing for fifty or so paces and then something would go wrong and they would all go back to the starting point and repeat the exercise. All of this was overseen by a drone flying overhead. I stood and watched for ages.

I had some time before the entry slot stated on my Hermitage ticket so I went back to the hostel for a comfort break and then, since the kitchen was empty, took my ukulele there for a quiet strum. Out and back in Palace Square again I found a Tourist Information kiosk so I asked there about the programme for the Victory Day activities. The staff didn't seem over-knowledgeable but were able to give me a little information. Turning away from there I walked the length of the square and past the main Hermitage museum entranceway, with a long slow-moving queue already forming, and past the closed entrance with its ten strongmen holding up the canopy. I didn't need either of those entrances. Instead, I went to the far end and into the entrance there. I showed my e-ticket at the desk, was given a plan of the museum and then led through airport-like security with my drawstring bag scanned and my person screened by the metal detector gate. Then without any more waiting I was in! It was all so quick and efficient.

The Hermitage is absolutely huge and to enjoy it to its full could easily take at least two or three days. Part of the museum is housed in the Winter Palace. This palace was built by Peter the Great between 1711 and 1712 and was then reordered by him in the 1720s. The Empress Anna commissioned Rastrelli to rebuild an adjacent palace to also include the Winter Palace. Rastrelli then rebuilt the palace a second time in the early 1750s for the Empress Elizabeth and the green and white finish he gave it is the external form that remains today, although the interior has had several redesigns. The Palace Square outside was the scene of the Bloody Sunday massacre of workers on 22 June 1905 that sparked the 1905 revolution.

I set off and decided to start at the top of the museum and work my way down. As I found the staircase that would take me upwards I realised that I was going against the flow of the many, many tour parties. However, looking determined and facing them down I made progress. There was so much to look at but I spent most of the time admiring the building itself and especially the chapel and the magnificent Jordan Staircase.

After a couple of hours of constant walking around the museum and avoiding other visitors I was getting tired and had had enough and was ready to rest and move on so I went back to the Jordan Staircase and down to the pretty internal courtyard and through this to the exit. Outside in the Palace Square again I was surprised to find it full of motorbikes, crammed full, with more arriving every moment. I wandered around admiring the bikes and then went the long way back to the hostel, past the Church of the Saviour on Spilled Blood, steeple jacks suspended on swing seats busily working on the outside, and with its adjacent stalls selling all sorts of tourist souvenirs. I spent a long time admiring the matryoshki dolls which were of many different sizes and qualities. I saw one that I thought would be a lovely gift for my wife until I realised I had miscalculated the price tenfold. The pictures on it were exceptional and I am sure it was worth the asked for sum but I only had the money I had.

Back at the hostel the different sleeping patterns in the dormitory were evident with the Aussie just getting up. He was young and probably needed to recover from a hard night's clubbing.

By this time it was mid-afternoon and time to go back to Nevsky Prospect and the metro down to the Alexander Nevsky monastery at the far end of the Prospect, nearly two miles away. However, I couldn't get to the metro station on the other side of the road since all the motorbikes from the palace square were now, with a police escort, parading very noisily down that road and the parade went on and on and on and they just kept coming. There were big bikes, small bikes, three wheeled bikes and bikes with side cars. In fact, every sort of bike of which one could think. I didn't catch the beginning of the procession but what I did see until the end lasted half an hour.

Eventually I was able to cross the road and caught the metro from Gostiny Dvor metro station, the interchange station with Nevsky Prospect, south east to Ploshchad Alexandra Nevskogo station and recrossed the road to the monastery. This monastery dates from the beginning of St Petersburg, having been founded in 1710. From the name of the Prospect and the monastery one can tell that Alexander Nevsky is a person of significance and he is a well-known figure from early 'Russian' history who lived in the thirteenth century. He was born in 1220 in Pereslavl-Zalessky north-east of Moscow and became Prince of the independent state of Veliky Novgorod. As such he defeated the Swedes, Germans and Estonians and for this protection of Orthodoxy against Roman Catholicism he is considered a great hero by the Russians. However, in 1248 he received the nominal lordship of Kiev under the authority of the Mongols and then in 1254 became Grand Prince of Vladimir on the same basis. In 1259 he acted on behalf of the Mongol Golden Horde in forcing Veliky Novgorod to pay tribute to them. He died in 1263.

Several male and female beggars of various ages and degrees of destitution were gathered around the entrance to the monastery. Going through them the monastery is approached down an alleyway with high brick walls each side behind which are graveyards with the remains of several famous people among the occupants. I spent quite a time walking around these, finding the famous departed and looking at the various monuments, some large, some small. Entrance to the monastery itself is free but priests stand in the gateway trying to take a fee for admittance. I ignored them and went in, making sure I complied with the sign with picture symbols that basically said 'no photos, no smoking, no 'phones, no dogs, no hats - women to wear head scarves - and definitely no shorts'. Once inside I was faced with more graves in the monastery grounds.

Walking into the monastery church I found this very busy, with people bowing and scraping to icons and crosses, including some Old Believers, with the ladies in red skirts down to the ground and arms and heads covered. A woman gave a black robed priest her baby and he then disappeared with the infant behind a screen and reappeared a couple of minutes later, a photograph was duly taken by the lady and the baby then handed back to her. I couldn't work out what that was all about. All through the church there was a lot of tinkling bell-ringing going on and that made it seem more Buddhist than Christian. I moved on elsewhere in the monastery complex, saddened at the feeling that I had witnessed a people in bondage to mysticism. After looking at several areas, including the bell ensembles on the ground, I paid to climb the bell tower, probably at a premium rate since the Russians in the queue in front of me showed ID cards before getting in. At the top of the tower a priest was busy sounding the bells while I admired the view.

Being in that area of St Petersburg I moved on from the monastery and walked, quite a long walk, along the Neva river bank to what I was expecting to be a museum but seemed to be government buildings and which were secured with vehicle barriers and guards and obviously not for public access. Nearby the normally bright blue painted Smolny Cathedral was completely covered in scaffolding and was pitch dark inside and so was disappointing. As I emerged from there back into daylight and my eyes adjusted to the bright sunshine again I gathering myself together and set off for the well laid-out and beautiful Tauride Park with its lake and the adjoining Tauride Palace, built by Catherine the Great for her lover Potemkin and the home of the State Duma between 1906 and 1917, but only saw the outside, with no public access permitted there either, before finding Chernyshevskaya metro station to take me back to Ploshchad Alexandra Nevskogo station. I had a reason for going back. I bought myself a Big Mac and a drink, both badly needed, at the McDonald's in the shopping centre adjacent to the metro station, and then went to the first supermarket I had found that we in the United Kingdom would recognise as such, and located in the same centre. As I expected I had to leave my bag in a locker outside and a kind security guard explained how that worked, with a bar code printed out on a receipt to allow me to retrieve my bag when I left. There I bought some healthy food including fruit and got some more bottled water. I had to do that in two attempts since when I first took the fruit to the cashier I hadn't weighed and bagged it and stuck on a bar code and so, to the disgust of the cashier, I abandoned those at the till, paid for everything else, put my purchases in the locker and then went back to buy the fruit properly.

I headed back to the hostel, noticing how many of the military were now around. I booked a cooked breakfast for the next day and then, leaving my food safely stowed away, I went out for the sake of it. As the evening went on I got myself a coffee in my insulated mug at the hostel and took that with me to listen again to the buskers. The crowd around these were singing along as before and also dancing. I just stood and listened but did manage to tap my foot from time to time. On several occasions I moved around to avoid smokers of whom there were many and especially women. One man, unusually, was smoking a pipe. At one point a nearby rubbish bin caught fire, presumably from a cigarette butt. Further down the Prospect was a bagpiper, not Scottish or Irish bagpipes but pipes from elsewhere and making a decent sound. Later, sitting in the hostel kitchen I enjoyed a last-of-the-day coffee, checked what I would need for the next day and counted how many roubles I had left.

I slept well, although vaguely aware of more comings and goings in the middle of the night and when I awoke at about half past seven on the Sunday morning there were now five of us in the dormitory. I showered, had a relaxed breakfast of my cornflakes and the pre-ordered and cooked one, again reheated in the microwave, and a coffee and then left just before half past nine to go on the metro to the suburb of Ozerki. Ozerki is principally blocks of flats, as are most of the suburbs around St Petersburg. The efficient metro took me to the right station, decorated with green mosaics of trees on the floor and walls, and I emerged from underground into bright sunshine. Looking at my map and walking past a couple of large lakes where the locals were fishing and sunbathing, I found what I was looking for.

Ozerki Baptist Church, one of the very, very few Protestant congregations in St Petersburg, has as its home what appeared to be an old Orthodox church which must have been redundant. The building still retains its onion dome however. Being a little bit early for the service I stood outside for a while at a distance, watching as people began to trickle in but eventually joined those, was welcomed, my 'good morning' identifying me immediately as a foreigner. As I went through the porch an older man responded with broken English and shook my hand and explained that he was a fourth generation Baptist and that his grandfather had been a pastor. However, any denomination other than Orthodox is still very rare in Russia and nowadays frowned on by the authorities and subject to ever increasing restriction of their activities. On the other side of the porch I found, about half way back, a discrete seat among the rows of chairs, with reasonable visibility of the hexagonal-shaped end section with its large cross on the end wall and the words 'Christ is Risen' and from where the service would be led and the choir participate. For a church where congregational participation was expected, with no separate priests' area, contrary to Orthodox services, the building had an ungainly and impracticable shape. Slowly the building filled and a family came in and sat in my row. We welcomed each other but the man then went to a different part of the building and brought back with him a young couple, the girl, his daughter, being about twenty years' old and an English speaker. That was very kind of him and as the service started I had translation. It was the end of their Easter celebrations and so the service started with a congregational response 'Christ is Risen', delivered three times. There was singing, some hymns recognisable to me such as Blessed Assurance, songs performed by the male and female robed choir, there was an interview to do with a drink and drugs addiction programme that the church ran, and a testimony from a man who had been in prison and was on the programme and whose mother was a church member, as well as a sermon delivered by the minister. As I took out my own Bible, very small for ease of packing, the tiny text of which I could only read two inches from my nose, I noticed sadly that few other members of the congregation had brought Bibles. After the sermon there were the usual church notices including an advertisement for a children's summer camp. The service lasted about two hours, longer than I expected, but that seemed the normal length and no one seemed to mind.

At the end of the service the family next to me and I chatted.

They very kindly invited me to their home but I explained that I was going to go to the Peter and Paul Fortress, which they didn't understand. 'Petra Pavlosk' I said. That did make sense to them. I gave the son, who must have been about ten years old, a fridge magnet of London and thanked the daughter for her English. 'Have you been to Britain?' I asked. 'No', she said. 'I learned my English as a student'. She learned very well. There were no refreshments afterwards so I left for the metro station and got on the most crowded train I had experienced so far in Russia, crowds that I would liken to those in London's rush hour. I successfully changed lines twice and got off the train at the Ploshchad Lenina metro station and went through Ploshchad Lenina, that is Lenin Square, unsurprisingly with a Lenin statue, in front of the rebuilt Finlandia train station, the place where Lenin had returned from exile. The fountains in the square suddenly started working as I was walking around and brought the square to life with their different timings and heights.

From there I had quite a long walk past the Samsonievsky Cathedral and on to the historic cruiser Aurora, which reportedly had fired the first shot of the October 1917 revolution from its guns and is now a museum ship. However, it was gone! All that was there was an empty mooring. I looked and checked and found a sign confirming that I was in the right place. I had been looking forward to seeing around the ship but couldn't if it wasn't to be found. Eventually I asked a nearby couple who told me it was being refitted in Kronstadt, the naval dockyard for the Baltic Fleet on the outskirts of St Petersburg, and would not be back in its place until June. I was disappointed but that would give me a good reason for a future return visit to the city.

Putting my disappointment to one side I strode firmly on with determination, admiring the white, blue and red flags lining the Troitskiy Bridge, past the brick cabin occupied by Peter the Great when he was building the city, relocated from elsewhere, and arrived at the Peter and Paul Fortress with a tourist helicopter buzzing overhead. This fortress was built by Peter the Great as a garrison citadel and a prison for political offenders and served as this until the 1917 revolutions. For a short time after it continued as a prison but in 1924 became a museum. As with a lot of St Petersburg it was severely damaged in the Second World War and has been restored. There was no entrance fee for the fortress, only for certain buildings within it. I walked over a bridge across the moat and started to look around the large complex. It is a fascinating place to visit with its fortifications and the Peter and Paul cathedral with its very, very tall and thin gold coloured spire and containing the tombs of Peter the Great and other Romanovs, including those of the fairly recently interred Czar Nicholas II and his wife Alexandra and their children. I spent over an hour there looking around the fortifications and observing the local population sunning themselves on the small beach beneath the fortress walls, before moving on elsewhere. As I did so I admired the Winter Palace and Admiralty buildings across the river, then went by the large mosque, decorated with turquoise tiles, passed by the rostral columns and eventually over Palace Bridge and back to the hostel to relax for a while and to freshen up. So far it had been a good day but, as ever, very hot.

A little while later, rested and energy returned, I was off again to the metro, this time to Moscovskaya station which was within a ten minute walk of the large Heroic Defenders of Leningrad war memorial set beneath road level in the middle of a roundabout and with eternal flames, flowers, plaques and dramatic statues and frescoes and also with rubber tiled floors which made the whole area eerily quiet. It is positioned at the furthest point of the German advance into St Petersburg, then Leningrad, in the Second World War or the Great Patriotic War as it is called in Russia, and was a moving reminder of the sacrifices of the city's people. As I left and got onto the metro again police were on the platform checking the papers of a dark skinned man, maybe yet another Chechen. I came out of Nevsky Prospect metro station and did two things. First, I bought an A3 size Russian flag from a street hawker so as to be ready for the Victory Day parade tomorrow and then, secondly, I had a McDonald's. Back at the hostel again I e-mailed home, relaxed and watched YouTube, both on my tablet, and had a quiet ukulele strum. I thought I would be alright doing that, with the hostel being largely empty at that time of day, but I got caught in the act - someone else appeared and listened in. They didn't run away so that was a comfort to me. Having more of the food I had bought the day before and a coffee I had my usual evening entertainment of listening to the groups in the Prospect and also watching a conjurer perform. Then I went and admired the missile launchers lined up in a side street and guarded by soldiers ready to the next day's parade. It was still not fully dark at eleven o'clock when I went back to the dormitory, which was empty, with the other guests still out and about. I showered and went to bed.

THE DAY OF THE BIG PARADE

I SLEPT WELL AND didn't hear the other dormitory occupants come in but am sure that was well, well after midnight. I woke up early but stayed resting in bed until about a quarter past seven when I decided to move and get into whatever awaited me that Monday, my last full day.

I had the breakfast I had ordered, reheated yet again in the microwave, and then, making sure I had a bottle of water with me, went up towards Palace Square for the Victory Day celebrations, joining a mass of other people heading in the same direction. However, everyone was being diverted away from the Square, which was reserved for guests, with ticket entry only, and towards the Admiralty building. The place I had mentally picked yesterday as a good viewing point wasn't accessible. In the end I found myself on the approaches to the Palace Bridge, on the opposite side of the road to the Winter Palace, and in the second row of people behind the crowd barriers and out of sight of whatever happened in the Square, but able to see all the parade on its way out. In the circumstances it was as good a place as I could have got and so I stayed. As ever there was an amount of waiting but then the sound of the parade starting reached our ears with bands, public address announcements, shouts of 'oorah' from the gathered soldiers and then, as military vehicles left the Square after doing their bit they passed by almost within touching distance - missile launchers, new tanks, old T-34 tanks, jeeps and so on as well as squads of soldiers. As all of this was going on police were busy checking the papers of anyone who looked suspicious, by which I mean Chechen types, and they took one away.

As things finished around mid-day the crowd started dispersing and I bought yet another large bottle of water and an ice cream and went back to the hostel. I chatted with the receptionist Veronica and she said there had been a parade on the river as well but I missed that. Nevertheless, I was very content with what I had seen. Veronica told me that the next event was the Veterans' Parade up Nevsky Prospect at three o'clock. When that time came I was ready, flag in hand and, keeping well away from the vans holding the blue camouflaged OMON interior ministry riot police, with their big black boots and thuggish appearance, I took my place, blending in with a crowd which was forming behind rope barriers along the pavement kerb. I think I was the only foreigner there. Then the parade started. There were marching soldiers in their dress uniforms, some holding red banners aloft and all goose stepping along. Then came the bands, the vintage jeeps and trucks carrying veterans, then groups of walking veterans and veterans pushed in wheelchairs and then giant flags carried horizontally by many, many marchers. Next were groups in traditional costume, and then, for an hour and a half, a procession of people holding up photographs of those killed in the war. It was all very moving, very tribal and I began to understand the heart of the Russian soul. It was like being an uninvited gate crasher at a family party. The rope barriers were supervised by young cadets, military I think, who were not very effective and at one point a police woman stepped in and was telling a family sitting on the kerb that actually they needed to move off the kerb. They decided to argue the point and the police woman gradually became more and more assertive and it appeared that they were a hair's breadth away from being arrested. However, they did eventually move. As the parade ended a drunk vagrant threw a bottle into the middle of the road where it broke with a loud smashing sound. Fortunately for him no one in authority saw from where it had originated. Gradually the marchers drifted wearily back home down the Prospect.

    I called back to the hostel, ordered for the next day what would be my last breakfast and then, in the early evening, joined the crowds in Palace Square to listen to a concert of war time songs and other music performed by singers and dancers on a raised stage. The Russians loved it and sang and jigged along and I'm sure it was well performed but to my ears it was dire. I stayed a little while and then slipped away.

With this being my last day I had to pack so I spent time at the hostel emptying all my bags and refilling them ready for the journey back home tomorrow. Then, as dark fell, it was time for the fireworks. Originally I thought that these were in the Square as well but on checking the programme I had been given by the Tourist Information kiosk I saw that these were actually being let off at the Peter and Paul Fortress and so headed out to position myself on the embankment behind the Winter Palace, leaning against the palace wall and looking over the water past the rostral columns, now with flames at their head, towards the launch point. I was early but as it turned out fortuitously so. After another half an hour the embankment was really crowded and it seemed as if the whole city had turned out to watch. The sky was not fully dark and it was not yet night when the first firework went up. The display only lasted thirty minutes but was very good. That over the crowd slowly, very slowly, but peacefully, shuffled away, some elements singing and dancing as they went. I let myself be carried by the masses as they all headed in one direction, the direction I wanted to go, down Nevsky Prospect, and I was able to peel off at Kazan Cathedral for the hostel.

When I got back to the hostel Uri was there. He didn't say where he had been in the intervening days but he was only in St Petersburg for one night before flying to Brussels tomorrow and then driving to Holland to continue his work.

My last night's sleep in St Petersburg was good and I woke up on the Tuesday morning refreshed. After a shower and dressing I had my good pre-ordered breakfast, as ever reheated yet again, and finished off with my remaining cornflakes and more of my milk kept in the hostel fridge. I went for a stroll around the nearby park behind the Kazan Cathedral and already found the day hot. I had to keep a close watch on the time and so it wasn't long before I returned to the hostel, finished packing, said thank you to the cleaner who kept everything very clean, and gave her a London fridge magnet, and then signed out, returning keys and fob and getting my locker key deposit back. I was pleased with my choice of accommodation which was very central, equipped with everything I found I needed, had a decent sized locker and was clean. The staff were friendly and helpful. However, now it was time to go. Luggage in hand I walked down the stairs for the last time, through the metal outside door, through the building archway, paused and looked once more from where I stood at the Kazan Cathedral, the Singer Building and the Church of the Saviour on Spilled Blood and then, with a spring in my step, satisfied at a successful, relaxed and fun few days, crossed Nevsky Prospect and used my last metro counter to go down the escalator to the platforms of Nevsky Prospect station. I surfaced at Moskovskaya station, found the right bus stop for the airport but didn't stay there. I had one last mission to carry out.

Crossing the road I headed into the back streets to the nearby Chesme Church. This was built by Catherine the Great in the late 1770s to celebrate the Russian naval victory against the Ottomans at the place of that name, Chesme in the Aegean Sea, and built at the place where she heard that news. Under the communists it was used as a labour camp and store house before being returned to the Orthodox Church in 1991. A service was going on inside with a robed, bearded priest swinging incense around, the smoke lingering and filling the air, and with candles being sold to worshippers young, middle aged and old, male and female, by the entranceway shop, and with some chanting going on. Not going in I instead went around the outside of the building, admiring its clean vertical patterns and the neat regular rows of graves, some with a military red star. Tower cranes were busy behind the church building something or other, possibly at the hospital located there or more flats. As I returned to the bus stop I walked past the boarded up eighteenth century Chesme Palace, also built by Catherine the Great as a way stop between St Petersburg and Tsarskoe Selo.

Back at Moskovskaya I had my airport sign ready for boarding the bus but actually took a marshrutky, which came along first, and paid the driver. This was crowded and I had to stand which I'm not sure was legal but it got me where I wanted.

The airport had a security check before entry into the building - everything into trays and through the scanner and me through the metal detector gate. Once that was successfully completed I booked in at the British Airways desk and got my boarding card. A waiting mother nearby was struggling to entertain her two young children, maybe three or four years old, so I gave each of them a fridge magnet, my last, to distract them for a while which seemed to work for the minutes I was there. Then it was through border control with my landing card taken, and through a second security process before reaching the cafes and shops in the airport lounge. I checked the departure board and the gate locations before getting myself a Burger King coffee at an inflated price, but using up most of my remaining rouble coins, and then sat down in the reasonably busy waiting area, among the bags and cases of other passengers, to quietly wait for the gate to be called. When the time came I was ready and knew in what direction to head and with a last passport and boarding card check I was welcomed aboard an A321 Airbus.

The flight was uneventful and unsociable with the person next to me engrossed in their own thoughts. There was on flight food of which I didn't have a clue what I was eating but it went down alright. I read and dozed, regretted that I had not been longer in St Petersburg to see so many unvisited sights, and in particular regretting missing the raising of the bridges on the Neva which happens in the early hours every summer and autumn night to allow ships through, and then settled down to draft various reviews to put on Trip Advisor when I was back. We landed at London Heathrow on time. After taking a little while to disembark I got quickly to border control and then, with no hold luggage, went straight through customs, all without incident, and eventually found the Piccadilly Line underground station and headed to Leicester Square, walked the familiar route from there to Charing Cross and caught a train home. As I sat in the train's carriage I realised that I had not thought of work at all and had just spent six stress and anxiety free days, each full of magnificent sights, all interesting, as well as the enjoying the ordinary, and that I had had a very special, very relaxed time.

So where next?

THE ADVENTURE THAT GOT AWAY

TRAVEL TO WILDERNESS RUSSIA

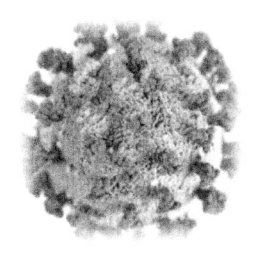

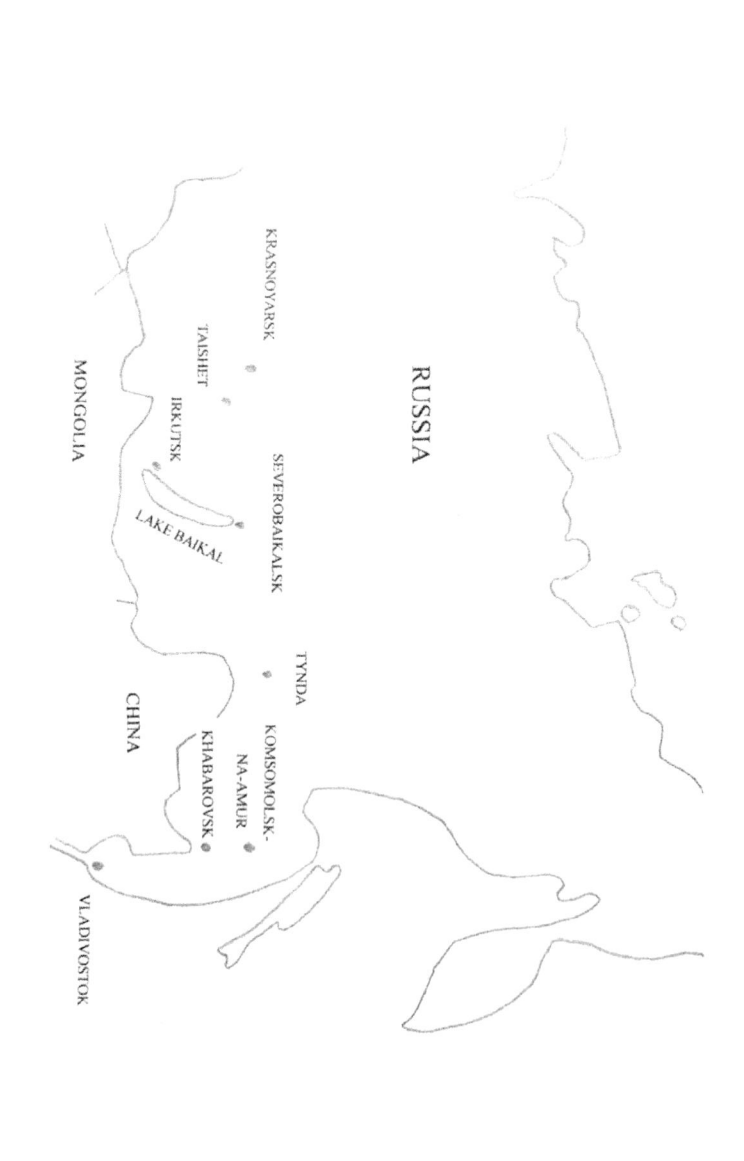

A WHIMPER

HOW DOES ONE CELEBRATE a significant birthday? These milestones only come every so often, usually every ten years, and are an excuse to do something different. The internet is full of suggestions for ways to celebrate. Things such as a family meal are always a nice idea. Some people are more lively and will hold a wild party. Others are daring and decide to do a parachute jump, go motor racing, have flying lessons, maybe a hot air balloon trip or something like that. Still others will find those ideas not to their taste and opt for a gentler activity such as wine tasting, a weekend away, an afternoon tea, a murder mystery evening or a cruise.

Having survived my various mid-life crises I allowed the years to drift by. During those years and after my trip to St Petersburg I travelled 'Clare-style' to other places in Eastern Europe including Ukraine, the Baltic states and Belarus. Now a new stage of my life was beckoning to me. In 2020 I would break out of my fifties and into the next decade. I would be sixty years old, sixty years having flashed by and the adventures I had enjoyed in the last ten years being the best of my life.

For over a year before this approaching significant event I wondered how I should celebrate. My wife, also approaching sixty, wanted us to have a joint wild party together, as wild as one can get at such an age, but that wasn't quite my scene. A wild party was had, and I played my part organising that, but for the celebration of only her sixtieth birthday. As I considered the options in front of me I realised that actually such a momentous event as a sixtieth birthday was a good excuse, as good as excuses come, for tackling 'the big one'. However, would that really be possible?

Typically, I kept my thoughts to myself as I pondered this during the Spring of 2019. There was no point revealing my hand too early. In quiet moments I searched a few headings on Google.

I popped into my local travel agent to see if they had anything useful but that exercise was unsuccessful. Next, I searched the house and finding the books I wanted settled down in my lunchtime breaks from work for a good read of my Lonely Planet Russia book and the Bryn Thomas book. Searching harder on my more remote home bookshelves I found my copy of 'The Siberian BAM Guide' by Athol Yates and Nicholas Zvegintzov and blew the dust away and opened that up. This last was the most useful book for me, useful for it was there where I had set my sights on going. Regardless of what others would think, whether my wife, family or friends, I thought and had decided that doing the BAM would be a good way to celebrate being sixty.

The BAM railway or, to give it its full name, the Baikal Amur Mainline, departs from the Trans-Siberian Railway at Taishet, situated west of Lake Baikal, then goes over the northern tip of that lake before heading eastwards, three or four hundred miles above the Trans-Siberian line, finally terminating at the Pacific Ocean at Sovetskaya Gavan. In doing so it passes through several substantial mountain ranges and very remote and inhospitable wilderness, as remote and inhospitable as anywhere in the world.

The BAM was conceived by the Soviet regime in the 1930s when it was realised that the Trans-Siberian Railway, the only effective link between the western and eastern parts of the USSR, was vulnerable to attack and could be easily cut, whether that be by the Chinese or the Japanese expanding into China at that time, or by others as happened in the Russian Civil War when American and British forces advanced with the Japanese out of Vladivostok. Therefore, the primary reason d'etre for the BAM was military. Work started under Stalin who used the sections built to service the Gulag system of prison camps and also used the inmates of that system to do the building. However, the eastern military threats to the USSR diminished and in 1941 work on the railway was suspended, except for the section at the extreme eastern end where the area had become, since 1930, heavily industrialised. Alongside the military justification for the BAM there was a realisation of the economic benefits such a railway could bring with access to untapped mineral and other natural resources.

As tensions between the Soviet Union and China increased in the late 1960s plans for the BAM were dusted off and some construction work started but it was only after 1974 that Brezhnev, the President of the USSR, pushed the project through using incentivised, some would say coerced, student 'volunteers.' The main line was completed in 1984. However, whilst the BAM was the world's largest single civil engineering project of the second half of the twentieth century, it has not lived up to its expectations. It has not generated prosperity, has had an adverse environmental effect on the area through which it passes and is increasingly considered to be a 'white elephant'.

I was amazed at myself for even considering such a trip as this but, even with my growing self-assurance and mastery of my fears and anxieties and my greater experience and confidence in travelling, I knew that I could not do this 'Clare-style'. This was not Moscow or St Petersburg. This was the outback of Russia, occupied by wild animals and wild men and I knew from the start that I wouldn't be able to do this on my own. It was too far away and too remote not to know exactly what was what. Also, a self-organised journey on the BAM would take too long for my mental health to hold up, hearing only Russian and not properly communicating with anyone, and would be very stressful with different flights and many trains needing to be perfectly coordinated. Some people would be able to do it, and do, but my nerves and my competence were not up to that. Instead, I would need to do this as some form of organised tour.

Somewhere at home I knew I had a pile of various papers in a folder, as we all do, but could not remember where. It took lots and lots of searching and more searching in all the corners of my house as well as in boxes stacked away in wardrobes full of the stuff of life until I eventually found the pile of papers for which I was looking. Even then I had to search right through that pile but towards the bottom I found what I wanted. That treasure was a quote JGR had given me back in 2014 for a bespoke solo tour of the BAM. I smoothed out the folds and creases from the paper and reread it with interest but interest only. JGR would organise a tour for me but not in a party. My reservations then about travelling alone remained now, so having refreshed my memory I did note that the quote was for the places to which I still wanted to go. I was being consistent. I made a few scribbled observations and then returned the quote to its place at the bottom of the pile of papers at the back of a wardrobe. I would now start looking for a group tour.

So it was back to spending more of my quiet moments searching online, sitting in front of the family PC with pen and paper for note taking on one side and a mug of tea on the other and blocking anyone else from using the machine. My efforts produced a couple of good results, Regent Holidays and Intrepid, although the Intrepid trip wasn't prominently listed on their main website but hidden away on an obscure site menu. Unlike the main Trans-Siberian route these were the only two providers I could find and these providers were both only offering tours bi-annually. This just shows the remoteness of the BAM and how far off the principal tourist trails it is.

Fortunately for me both Regent and Intrepid intended to run tours in 2020 lasting roughly two weeks. Both would be group tours, with minimum and maximum group numbers given, the range being three up to sixteen. Programmes and stops were roughly the same. Flights and visa would need to be clarified. I looked at the advertised cost of each and Intrepid gave the less expensive better price without flights and visa. However, Intrepid are based in Australia but I knew someone who had used them to go elsewhere in the world and they had been happy with them.

So as 2019 moved into Spring I decided to have a chat with a good-sized travel agent, Flight Centre, since if I went with Intrepid not only were they based in Australia but I would need to sort out my own flights to and from the tour's start and end points. I would rather use an agent to take that responsibility. When I visited my local Flight Centre they presented as competent and good and had ATOL protection but I did have to show them where Intrepid had hidden the tour on that company's website. Bookings for this weren't open at that point in time but I walked away with a reasonable idea of budget including for flights, which I could afford, and a date to put in my diary for when I could book. In the meantime my wife again tried to persuade me to join her and have a joint sixtieth birthday party instead of going on another trip, as if her attempts would ever succeed!

I returned to Flight Centre on the date booking opened, 3rd August 2019, which I had put in my work diary and underlined in red in my home diary so as not to miss it. After all, the maximum number for the trip was sixteen and I would hate to be number seventeen and turned away. In fact, I think I was number one. Armed with my passport and payment card I walked through Flight Centre's shop door, was offered a seat and then the process started. Flight Centre's agent went through the details with me, a tour in June 2020, starting in Vladivostok, a city with which I was familiar but seeing other sights, then to Khabarovsk, Komsomolsk-na-Amur, Tynda, Severobaikalsk and finally Krasnoyarsk. The standard of trains would be very similar to those on my first trip, on the Trans-Siberian.

For flights it was suggested that I go through Seoul in South Korea to get there but I put to Flight Centre that Moscow may be less expensive and it was. I would need to get a flight back from Krasnoyarsk which would also be through Moscow so I asked for two or three extra days in the Russian capital to have a look at places I hadn't yet seen such as the Kolomenskoye Palace, the Kremlin Armoury and the All-Russian Exhibition Centre.

After about an hour I had finished the booking process and walked out of the travel agent with a lighter bank account, a two hundred pound deposit having been paid to Intrepid to secure my place, and approximately six hundred and fifty pounds spent on flights booked from London Heathrow to Vladivostok through Moscow Sheremetyevo and from Krasnoyarsk to Moscow

Sheremetyevo and then three days later from Moscow Domodedovo to London Heathrow, all paid and with Aeroflot. The total overall cost was in the same region as my first adventure on the Trans-Siberian but I did get a five per cent discount through Flight Centre. Every penny helps. I had to pinch myself before I knew that I was going and hadn't just dreamt it.

I took out travel insurance that day with Direct Line and then, a month or so later, came the dreaded visa process.

My sister had recently been to St Petersburg and had successfully done her own visa application, which I found impressive, and anything she could do I must be able to do! Intrepid assisted the process as part of their package, using a Russian-based company acting as their agent for the trip, and who provided the Letter of Invitation and other documentation to support my own visa application. I had kept copies of my previous visa applications so knew the various answers I would need to give and I made sure I included extra days in Moscow in my dates. So, a couple of months after booking the trip, I got on the train and took the now familiar route up to Goswell Road and dropped off my completed forms, letter of invitation, passport and finger prints and paid the requested fee. A few days later I checked the progress report on the visa centre's website and was told that my passport with inserted visa could be collected, my preferred option rather than secure postage. So collect it I did.

And again, as always, I started printing off maps from Google and doing lists and more lists of what to take, checked my vaccinations and all the other usual preparations, leaving the getting of currency and a travel cash card until nearer the departure time.

The process had been easy, stress free, and I didn't feel that I was particularly going out of my comfort zone. The last task to complete was Intrepid's final payment, due on 27th March 2020.

Summer went by, autumn went by, Christmas came and went and a new year dawned. My excitement grew as each day saw my trip get closer.

In the middle of January 2020 one of my daughters fell ill with some form of chest infection and so my wife and I were called in to help care for her and for her own children. Over a period of ten days or so first her husband and then, since he was at work at the time, my wife and I separately had to take her to the local hospital's Accident and Emergency Department due to her having trouble breathing. The medics eventually diagnosed pleurisy and gave her medication although we didn't feel quite confident that they had got their diagnosis right. Anyway, thankfully over the next few days she recovered and we thought nothing more of it, just relieved that she could now look after her own children and we could have a rest! However, we now have a better idea of what she had.

We will all remember February 2020. News had been trickling through over the two or three previous weeks about a high mortality 'flu' like illness in China and then as time progressed there were reports of this appearing elsewhere in the world including Europe. At the very end of January a few cases were reported in the United Kingdom and the government health authorities decided that the best protection was to encourage everyone to wash their hands thoroughly while singing 'Happy Birthday' a couple of times - the traditional song and not the Stevie Wonder version - and to keep away from each other. However, in Italy the hospitals were unable to cope with the sudden influx of the very ill and people were dying in the streets. Another week or so passed and the exponential advance of the COVID pandemic became obvious to all. We, that is my wife and I, were sure that this had been circulating in this country in January and that was the mystery illness that floored our daughter.

As February gave way to March hospitals here were full to overflowing, the mortality rate was very high, emergency Nightingale hospitals were set up, and the pandemic was getting worse. Throughout the world travel was being shut down and countries were closing their borders.

The illness advanced and as it did so I followed as closely as I could what was happening in Russia but reliable and truthful information on that was in short supply. Officially they only had a few cases. Unofficially they were in crisis. At the back of my mind was the knowledge that medical care in Russian hospitals lacked the finesse of those in western Europe and doubts were beginning to creep in as to whether it was wise to go on my planned adventure, especially since I was in a vulnerable age group - just - and I would be travelling in poorly ventilated and crowded trains, ideal conditions for the spread of disease. What should I do?

I was in a real dilemma. I was due to pay the balance for the trip at the end of March. If I didn't pay the balance and instead cancelled I would lose my deposit and flight money. If the pandemic then faded away I would feel silly. If I decided to pay the balance and go what was the risk of falling ill and if I did would I survive Russian medical care? My own conclusion was that the risk of falling ill was great and I probably wouldn't survive a Russian hospital. If I paid the balance and then cancelled would I get any of my money back? Stress and anxiety swept over me. I read and reread my travel insurance terms and conditions as well as those from Intrepid and Aeroflot. I kept checking Foreign Office advice but that was no help at all. However, on 16th March the Russian government announced that it was closing its borders to foreigners as from 18th March. I breathed a huge sigh of relief. I had in fact gradually and very begrudgingly formed the view that going would not be at all sensible but decided to wait as long as possible in case things changed. Now I knew that they wouldn't change and the situation was clarified. I couldn't go. The Russian government was preventing me from going. I asked Flight Centre to cancel. They sorted out the cancellation with Intrepid, told me I may not get my flight money back and so I then put in an insurance claim for my flights at least. An e-mail and a letter went off to Direct Line to lodge my claim with costs to follow. I didn't expect to hear anything soon since I was very sure that my claim was only one of many, many thousands to hit their desks.

Then things got worse. On 23rd March the Prime Minister announced that the whole of the United Kingdom was going into lockdown in three days' time and suddenly a very different set of concerns around home working and isolation took over. One day I was working with colleagues from an office, the next day each of us had loaded our computers into our cars and taken them home. One day I could socialise with people face to face, the next only on Zoom. One day I could walk where I wanted and the next I could only get out once a day for exercise. One moment I could see and the next I was having to wear a mask and look out on the world through steamed-up glasses.

Not being able to go on the BAM hurt but I had to accept that my dreams were not going to be realised. Frustration was mixed with relief and I knew that I was in a much better position than others who had longed-for holidays cancelled. I accepted that I would lose some money but in reality my financial exposure was quite limited.

As with the rest of the high street Flight Centre no longer had a shop open for me to walk into and sit across a desk working out how to get my money back. All of that had to be done by e-mail and telephone. So at the same time that I was setting up an old kitchen table at home to take my work computer and keep my job going, as again did all of my colleagues and so many others, I was also trying to communicate with Flight Centre to see what costs I could recover.

Intrepid fairly swiftly advised that they would keep my deposit for use against future trips with them over the next couple of years, as their terms and conditions had said. I was not sure whether in these circumstances that was legally right or fair but they were based outside of English law, being in Australia, would already have spent some time on initial organising of the tour and so I accepted that as the best I could get. In the end I never did any other trips with Intrepid in that timescale so lost that money.

Flights were another matter. Flight Centre seemed to have a turnover of staff at that time which wasn't helpful. I don't know whether they had redundancies or put staff on furlough or whether staff left of their own accord. However, for me it meant that I was disempowered and completely in their hands. Sensible communication was non-existent, telephone calls were not possible and it was e-mail or nothing, often nothing with some e-mails returned as undelivered. One moment they said that I would get seventy per cent of my flight money back and at another moment they said they weren't sure and at yet another moment that they had no idea as to timescales for whatever money they could get. I don't think the airlines themselves knew what was going on either.

In the end I contacted Aeroflot directly who said that they would keep my money to use against other flights with them and if unspent after three years would then return it. However unsatisfactory that was it seemed the best deal on offer and I decided I would have to accept that. I slept on it for a couple of days and then just as I was preparing to take that offer Flight Centre came back to me and confirmed that all of the flight money had been returned to them and was going into my bank account. I kept checking until it duly arrived there and that was a huge relief and felt like a special birthday present all on its own! I advised Direct Line and withdrew my insurance claim.

But sadly my plans to further explore Russia ended with a whimper and not with a bang. Nevertheless, I was resolved that as soon as the pandemic abated, which thankfully with vaccines and variants it seemed to be doing as 2021 progressed, I would try for the BAM again, if not in 2022 then in 2024. Some chance. In 2022 another event emerged to stop me going. As 2021 approached its end it appeared that Russia was building up its troops in a threatening manner near the Ukrainian border and the West issued warnings to Russia to not even think of invading. Surely Putin must be bluffing? After all, this isn't the age when empires are made, and especially not by military force. However, on 24th February 2022 the unbelievable happened and Russia launched a ten day 'special military operation' with the aim of toppling the Ukrainian government, replacing it with a puppet regime and occupying at least half of that country. Eighteen months later the war is still going on and any tourist trip to Russia may be one way, straight to a Siberian prison, with no exit allowed. So my dream has died - but only for the time being. Realistically though this situation will pertain for the foreseeable future. I genuinely grieve for the good, kind people of both Russia and Ukraine, those I met on my travels and those I didn't meet, who only want to live in peace and have been caught up in Putin's evil, destructive war against their wishes and judgment. Peace will, at some point, come and we hope that that will be soon. Recovery, though, for both countries and their peoples, will take a lot, lot longer.

EPILOGUE

REFLECTIONS

THE FOUR JOURNEYS TO Russia that I actually completed expanded my horizons and ambitions in ways I could never have anticipated. At the age of fifty most people settle into a life of 'more of the same'. I have been thrilled to do otherwise. In terms of travel I am still a novice compared to so many others but I do not need to be competitive about that. I am content with what I have done, not only in Russia but now also elsewhere, and what I haven't achieved in volume I have achieved in quality. I have been where most do not go and thoroughly enjoyed it. However, alongside my physical journeys I have completed another journey, a journey from fear and hesitancy to boldness and confidence. Pushing my boundaries in travel has helped. Changing my job has helped. Yet in all areas of life I do have to actively manage my stress levels and that is the case whenever I pack my bags and head off to new destinations. Nevertheless, I am in a different place now to where I was.

I have broadened my horizons in the last few years to other countries in Eastern Europe and whilst I am in love with that whole area as well as with Russia, Russia is a particularly special place for me. As I have said before, it is a lovely country, with kind and generous people who aspire to the material and political lifestyle that we in the West enjoy. Sadly, its government is not of a similar mind.

On all my trips I now travel 'Clare-style' as much as I can and know that to do that I have to research and prepare, I have to remove the unknowns and not try to achieve the impossible, however tempting that may be. Some can travel without those preparations and I have every respect and admiration for them. I cannot. Fortunately, these days there are so many resources available to help plan, ranging from physical guide books to websites, to review sites such as Trip Advisor, to YouTube clips and to conversations with those who have already been and returned. All of these are incredibly useful. Of course, things can still go wrong. The wrong bus, the misreading of a train timetable, reversing a map or allowing insufficient time for connections can all be disastrous. However, knowing that means I can make plans to avoid such circumstances.

My hope is that, when the present war in Ukraine is over, a return to Russia will be possible and that others too will tread that path and see and experience what I have been privileged to see and experience. May that day come quickly.

PROFILE

LANDERS FARAWAY GREW UP in Beckenham in the United Kingdom and has always lived within reach of his childhood home. He was schooled in Beckenham and on leaving school started a career as a surveyor with his first job also based in his home town. He is now, only very recently, of an age when he can leave his surveyor's career behind and forge a new career, or rather careers, in retirement as a childminder for his expanding number of grandchildren, supplied by his three adult daughters, as a volunteer in a school and as a DIY 'expert' in his home. He has a very understanding wife.

Printed in Great Britain
by Amazon